To Die in Style!

To Die in Style!

The residential lifestyle of feasting and dying in Iron Age Stamna, Greece

Gioulika – Olga Christakopoulou

ARCHAEOPRESS PUBLISHING LTD
Summertown Pavilion
18-24 Middle Way
Summertown
Oxford OX2 7LG

www.archaeopress.com

ISBN 978-1-78491-935-1
ISBN 978-1-78491-936-8 (e-Pdf)

© Gioulika – Olga Christakopoulou and Archaeopress 2018

All rights reserved. No part of this book may be reproduced, or transmitted, in any form or by any means, electronic, mechanical, photocopying or otherwise, without the prior written permission of the copyright owners.

Printed in England by Oxuniprint, Oxford

This book is available direct from Archaeopress or from our website www.archaeopress.com

Contents

Preface and acknowledgments 1

Introduction 2

What we live by we die by Robert Frost 3

The Banquet through the Burial Testimony 4

Fare thee well. The Stamna Timeless Farewell 31

Feasting and Dying in a lebes; an institutional innovation with an international appeal 36

Symposium, Religion and Cult portrayed through successive layers of burials, (semi) circular constructions and pyres 37

'Consuming' with the dead 52

Old cities, old souls… 55

'In Darkness We Trust' 58

References 70

Preface and acknowledgments

The present paper is based on the results of my PhD research and on the rich recent literature on the subject, which now turns the attention not only to the typological analysis of the archaeological material, but mainly to its interpretative approach, treating the latter as an agent playing an active role, and thus reflecting the social structures of a particular society. In this instance I would like to express my gratitude to Dr. Marilena Tsakoumaki fellow archaeologist, for editing and improving the English text. Furthermore I would like to sincerely thank Mary Giamalidi MA, Dr Evy Papadopoulou, Dr Vassiliki Brouma and Dr Gregory Grigorakakis, also fellow archaeologists, but above all friends, for our discussions and the trust they have bestowed on me. I'm particularly grateful to Dr Georgia Z. Alexopoulou, Dr Christina Marini and Maria Golfinopoulou for they have decisively contributed to my study in all possible ways, while I wish to record a special debt of gratitude to Professor Thanasis I. Papadopoulos for reading my study and discussing the subject. It has benefited much of his wisdom.

Last but not the least, I would like to thank my husband Ioannis Somakos who has been organizing folders, photos and drawings for the last twenty-five years of our life with immense love, respect and patience. I couldn't have a better colleague experience...

Introduction

Symposium for the ancient Greeks was a kind of traditional ritual performed in the occasion of a social event.[1] It was governed by customary individual and collective rules and was accompanied by procedures and even objects which were very closely connected with the participants and the ceremonies, indicating more than just a reception/meeting with benefits, for the sole purpose of enjoying it. Several theories arise about the importance of *symposium* which, briefly and bearing in mind the well-known bibliography, it is said to have the purpose of ensuring the friendly relations between the participants and the participants themselves with the deities towards which they were often addressed. In addition, a symposium could be a moment of cohesion[2] where the social/military hierarchy was validated and legitimized,[3] even when it was part of the funeral process.

There are several synonymous words,[4] which more or less describe the concept of the process. In the burial process of Stamna perhaps the term ritual banquet could be better used in the sense of *'food and drink consumption'* as a result of the initial social process, which can be characterized as a domestic banquet but also as a symposium[5] or feasting.

As Wright claims[6] *'there is no generally accepted definition of feasting'* but for the purpose of writing his article, which refers to feasting in the Mycenaean society, he defines feasting as *'the formal ceremony of communal eating and drinking to celebrate significant occasions'*.[7] Supporting his view, and in order to specify the issue to be

---

[1] For the symbolic aspects of food consumption and how this process creates, maintains and defines social and political relations (in terms of an international In concept culture) see Sánchez Romero, Aranda Jiménez, Alarcón García 2007, with relevant bibliography.

[2] Corner 2015.

[3] Brouwers 2010, 239.

[4] With reference to Terminology also see, *'Festivals and Feasts, Greek.'* Ancient Greece and Rome: An Encyclopedia for Students, edited by Carroll Moulton, vol. 2, Charles Scribner's Sons, 1998, pp.65-67. World History in Context, (link.galegroup.com/apps/doc/CX2897200184/WHIC?u=tlc199095657&xid=b741b924), Accessed 23 Aug. 2017.

[5] For further references to the notion of symposium and to the first elements that establish it in historical times see Wekowski 2012, 19 ff., who refers extensively to the definition of the concept, to its historical origins, to its interpretation, and also to the ritual models occurring and distinguished by archaeological documentation (sympotic vessels etc), and finally to its presence in later periods. See also notes 3 &10 referring to the review of Murray's bibliography who dealt with the subject.

[6] Wright 2004, 133. For further definitions of the meaning of feasting, see also 2004 134-135. Studies of Borgna 2004 and Steel 2004, face the feasting process in Cyprus and Crete as a tradition, clearly characterizing the elite class of the settlements.

[7] Wright 2004, 133. In general, for the importance of feasting as an integral process in the socio-

analyzed, he argues that *'material evidence for either eating or drinking may indicate feasting, but one must scrutinize the evidence closely to determine whether the remains are the result of formal and ritual activities not involving feasting'*.[8] Among the references made on definitions that give the sense of feasting, he claims also that *'feasting is an important ceremony instrumental in the forging of cultural identity'*[9] and that *'the universality of its practice underscores its importance in the formation of identity'*.[10]

In the case of Stamna, the *symposium* both as a concept and as a process involving prominent citizens of the establishment, is documented mostly by the finding of the large cauldrons, the tripod jars and the tripod vessels. It should be emphasized that, as the process of *symposium* is presumed to be a social event, which when its owner was alive it accounted for a sufficient number of participants, it is also presumed by the *burial commodity* of the Stamna excavation, that in the burial process the number of participants had to be quite small, an issue which, as we shall see below, is still under discussion. In other words, in Stamna there may be a reverse ritual process where a burial practice consisted of (possibly) a limited number of participants, in contrast to a social event which included vice versa (i.e., in vivo), a remarkable number of attendants.

Regardless of the form of the whole process, the concept behind the formal ritual as part of the burial process bridged the gap between life and death, and constituted a meaningful way of communicating with the metaphysical, which was perceived (or at least would like to be treated) both at a personal and a social level, forming part of a perfectly normal and natural process.[11]

What we live by we die by. Robert Frost

Dealing with death and copying with grief by family and close relatives[12] is reflected through the treatment of the dead body, the location of burials and their accompanying objects. Body and Soul are interrelated and must be treated after death in the same way they are treated in life: as one. Therefore, ritual procedures aim at alleviating pain during the transition as well as preserving the enjoyment with the assistance of provisions which were necessary for them

---

political life of the Aegean world, especially in the 13th century, see Palaima 2004.
[8] Wright 2004, 133.
[9] Wright 2004, 134.
[10] Wright 2004, 135.
[11] See Dakouri-Hild 2016, 11-30, for a detailed literature on the concept and the manner in which the ancient people fully incorporated their everyday life into the funerary environment.
[12] For a sociological report of the importance of kinship and worship of ancestors of ancient Greek society see the noteworthy handbook of Numa Denis Fustel De Coulanges, *The Ancient City: A Study of the Religion, Laws, and Institutions of Greece and Rome*, Batoche Books, Kitchener 2001. (Reprint of the Lathrop, Lee & Shephard Co., Boston, 1873 edition).

when they were alive, and for the appeasement of the soul. Whether buried or surrendered to the fire, the dead had the same needs and the same rights, and for that reason the relatives had considerable time to perform specific rituals so that the dead could receive the necessary care. In Stamna, evidence of this care is summed up, among other in accompanying pyres for the on-site preparation of a funeral supper, the depositing of pouring and drinking vessels and the use of few but representative ritual vases with cuts in their base as an indication of their use. Also, the placement of personal objects, items of everyday use and armor either in the grave, or as an offer to cover pyres. For the same reasons and in similar ways, the findings of Stamna cemetery bear witness to the great interest of Body and Soul treatment of the deceased also with the celebration of festive events relative to those held when the deceased was alive and denote the use of burial household equipment as formerly functional.

Unfortunately, the lack of identified residential facilities[13] in the area of Stamna, with all the following elements that can, at least in this particular matter, relate to the consumption of goods both in public and private spaces, does not help towards the identification of devotional or other gathering places, so as to combine them with specific types of tripod (or other) vessels found in graves and related to ritual or common feasts. For the same reason, the up to date findings cannot safely refer either to the customary simple daily consumption, or to wider social in style periodic customs with the final purpose of expressing interest in a social / political / economic / military issue, or an event in which the participants sought among other things, to stabilize or imposing their views. Customs and events though, towards which we are directed by the denotation of the burial findings themselves.

The Banquet through the Burial Testimony

A. *The tomb evidence*

In all the up to date excavated and studied tombs, only the apsidal one (Figure 1) which was excavated in 1994, probably imitates an arched house of the early Iron Age and testifies to the architectural tradition which involves the construction of houses for the accommodation of the elite in the region of Stamna, forming thus the connecting link between the living and the dead through the banquet process. Moreover, the incorporation of the built bench on which vessels for pouring and drinking were disposed, reinforces the theory of the banquet process with the purpose of emphasizing the superiority of the deceased in bygone times, when as a host / landlord negotiated powerfully in

---

[13] Christakopoulou 2016, 62.

Figure 1. The monumental apsidal tomb with the libation bench. It is considered to be one of the earliest tombs of the ancient cemetery. It included four burials at different levels dating back to early Protogeometric times, with origins in the sub-Mycenaean period as evidenced by the typology of the urn vessels.

his territory. The use of benches and the arched portion of the house as a food preparation area is also testified in the arched house in Xeropolis,[14] Lefkandi, witnessing the powerful office of the dead for whom the tomb was built as a house effigy,[15] adding another common element to those that incorporate the society of Stamna into the corresponding, excavated and studied to date societies of the Early Iron Age.[16] One of the additional elements that support this view and relate to the same grave, is the identification of a large number of iron fragments on its pebbled floor and adjacent to the buried dead, for which primarily the tomb was constructed. Their identification with pin fragments is revised as it is more likely that the discovered multiple iron fragments belong to spits[17] (Figure 2) whose participation in household equipment for the elite is essential both for their usability and for their symbolic presence within the graves.

---

[14] Popham - Sackett - Themelis 1979, pl.8a. Popham - Sackett - Themelis 1980, 14.
[15] Crielaard 2016, 56-57.
[16] See Mazarakis Ainian 2009.
[17] For the use and presence of spits see Rethemiotakis – Egglezou 2010,176, pl.237a-b. In Stamna, the large number of iron fragments that remain unidentified due to their progressed fragmentary condition and oxidation, argue towards this interpretation.

In addition, the finding of a tripod pithos (Figure 3) inside the vaulted tomb with a burial function, indicates the initial use of pithos as part of household equipment which was used for the preparation of food of a festive nature and was further used after the death of one of the tomb owners/officials, acquiring an emblematic character.[18] Both the amphoras (Figure 4) that included cremation in different layers within the vaulted tomb, and whose mass presence increased the status of the tomb as a former funeral banquet locale, can be perceived as purely symposium vases.

As in the sum of the up to date excavated tombs[19], which exceeds 700 in number, no other such tomb has been found, this grave could be identified not only as the tomb of an official but as the tomb of the ruler / leader of the residential facility who first led his people to settle in the Stamna area. It is, perhaps, the one whom people trusted through the big and dangerous for all seasons journey, which was imposed on them under unknown circumstances[20] and which ended with the founding of a facility, as evidenced by the so far excavated necropolis, and which dominated the north east side of the lagoon Aetoliko towards the NW (Figure 5). Despite the adverse conditions certainly faced in an era that followed the destruction of the palaces and the wandering of extraneous populations, with which it is most likely that collided, he managed to lead them through known (or unknown) roads and install them safely in the area of Stamna, where rural prosperity and autonomy in terms of finding raw materials, helped the population to recover financially and to meet the requirements of the newly established facility. For this leader and founder, the inhabitants chose to build a tomb, investing time and money, architecturally inspired by the residential architecture of the leaders of the settlements of the period, as we already know, following the practice of inhumation. In this same tomb they chose to include the cremated dead associated with the original owner of the tomb not only biologically but also through their socio-political/military status, as members of the same social group, the elite. It is no coincidence that this particular dead was accompanied by spits[21] and a bent spear.[22]

---

[18] See Fox 2012, 59. Elements inside a tomb that testify to the performance of banquets are of symbolic character and enhance the ceremonial aspect of the ritual.
[19] The data occurring according to the latest publications.
[20] Christakopoulou 2016.
[21] Recently revised, see above n.17.
[22] A rare ritual, bearing in mind the burial practice of placing bent swords, Lloyd 2015, 20. According to the scholar this policy is not mentioned anywhere else before the end of the 8th century, except in Prinias Crete. Maran 2012, 125 (with respective bibliography) with regard to the bent swords of Tiryns states that, although the destruction they underwent may be due to prior use, however, rich indications of similar funerary ensembles in Central Europe of the late second and early first millennium, are consistent with their ritual destruction.

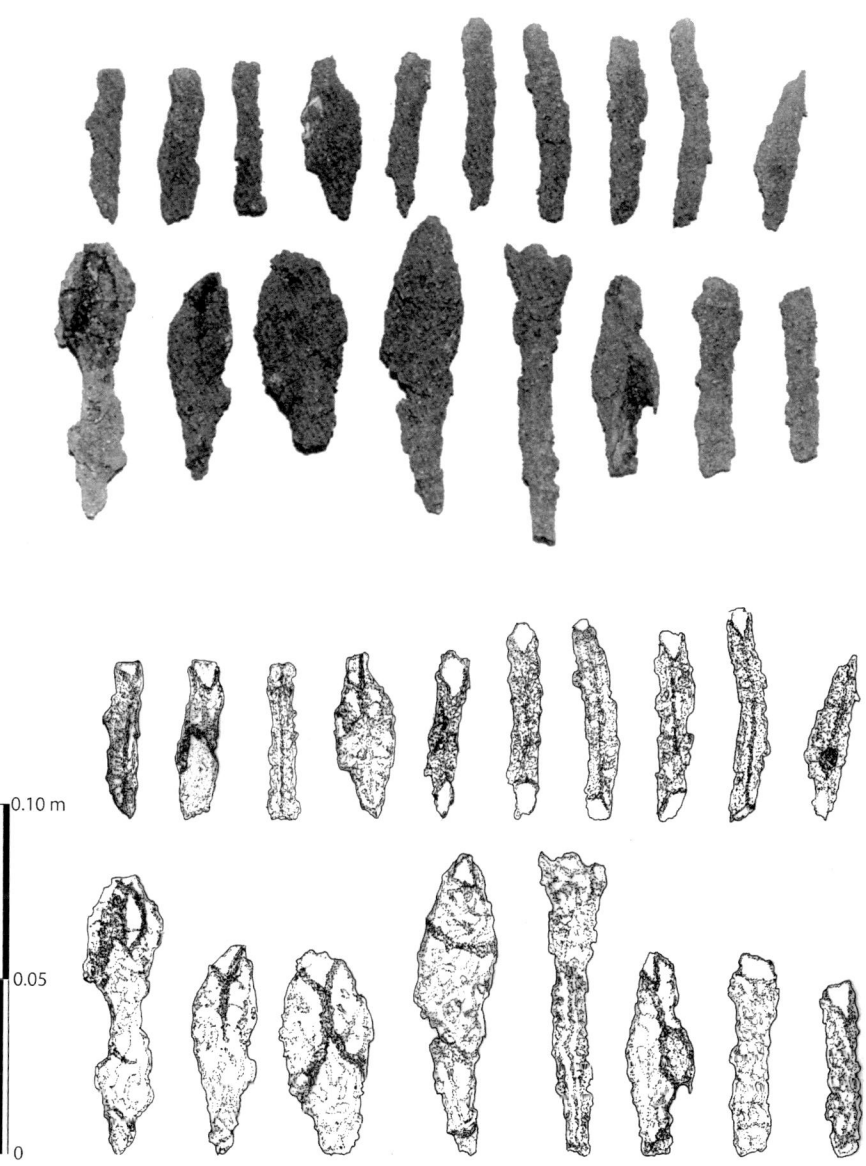

Figure 2. The quantity of fragments and the most recent literature on the recovery of similar objects in graves, leads to a revision of their interpretation, as it is safer to identify them as spits.

Figure 3. The clay tripod pithos KT2/94 that contained the remains of the last cremation placed within the apsidal tomb. An "enagismos" in honor of the dead is testified by the presence of two trefoil oinochoae and two other unidentified vessels.

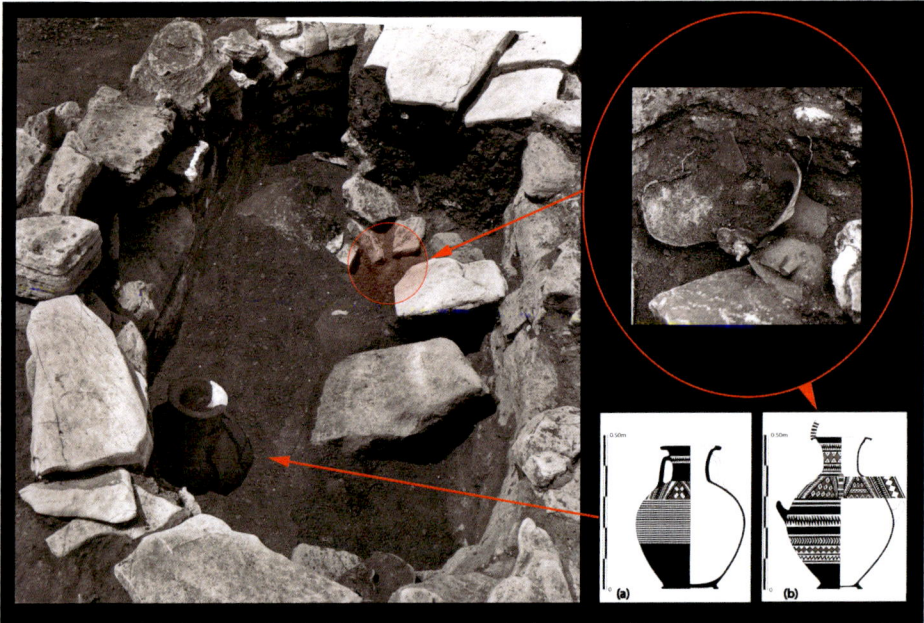

Figure 4. The two amphoras a.KT5/94, b.KT6/94, with the cremated remains inside the apsidal tomb. The types of amphoras and their decoration imitate Late Helladic standards. In addition, the shape of the KT6 vase is similar in terms of typology to protogeometric amphorae from Cyprus.

Figure 5. Google map of the Aetoloakarnania perfecture and the protogeometric sites. The neighboring positions of Achaia and Ithaca are noted because their populations exhibit typological similarities to those of Stamna.

It is no coincidence that this tomb contained the cremations of the dead in innovative constructions such as in a large tripod pithos and in an amphora (Figure 6) accompanied by insignia as for example the bent sword,[23] a spearhead and a shield boss, because the elite of this particular period and as evidenced also in the Stamna region, is intertwined with military policy.[24] And it is no coincidence that the urns and the findings accompanying burials[25] are original objects on all the finds of the cemetery with typological echoes in Cyprus and Italy,[26] elements that can be perceived as either commodities either as commuting products, perhaps in the form of both immigration and extramarital affairs. The purpose of their presence in this tomb may never be learned but the echo – whether true or invented – of a different cultural environment of total cluster graves and of the total of the cemetery generally, is real. Therefore they should be also discussed and considered under particular interpretative approach.

---

[23] About the deposition of bent or killed swords, the terminology used, and the exclusiveness of the rite, see Lloyd 2015.
[24] Brouwers 2010, 238.
[25] Christakopoulou 2001.
[26] For example, the four-handled burial amphora KT6, Christakopoulou 2009, 1118-1119, and the golden hair spirals KT10/94 and KT11/94, Christakopoulou 2009, 1281-1282.

10   To Die in Style!

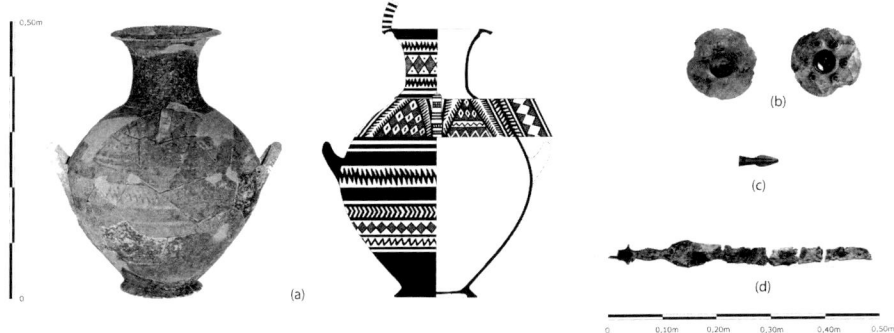

Figure 6. The amphora KT6/94 (a) which was accompanied by a shield boss (b), a spearhead (c) and a bent sword (d) as insignia dignitatis.

It becomes apparent that the tomb was not only constructed as the ultimate residence of the high prestige of dead (irrespective of their number – one or more) which he included, but at the same time as space into which the last formal ritual feasting symbolically occurred, as evidenced by the incorporation in the architectural composition of the apse and the built bench. The evidence of spits (provided the total over 80 iron and oxidized fragments are spits) along with their capacity in domestic use for roasting meat, accentuates the importance of *symposium* regarding the position of the deceased in the upper echelons of the hierarchy.[27] The whole hypothesis is enhanced by the subsequent placement of the amphorae and the tripod pithos whose dimensions are large and extremely disproportionate to the built tomb, and yet it was placed within it, in order to be included in the monumental (for that particular era) construction.

The burial site excavated in 1994 still represents the model of the dominant residence of the prominent (amongst others) settlement of Stamna, which was probably inhabited by the authorized hierarch, and furthermore by those who succeeded him and who, in the context of their politics carried out within the ritual or communal feasts.[28] And while one could speculate that not finding a similar construction leads to the conclusion that it was mere an echo of a specific architectural style, followed in the area from which the population originated, it is my personal belief that this house, which has been inhabited

---

[27] For the significance of the spits and their identification with symbols that belong to warriors and the elites in Cyprus, see Hamilakis- Sherrat 2012, 194-195 with relevant bibliography. For the reference of spits in Homer see Sherrat 2004, with all the relevant literature.

[28] For a similar theory on the use of the IV-1 house in Nichoria, see Fox 2012, 71; 68, fig.5.5. In the same chapter, Fox examines representative houses of the same period, in which apparent feasting data is present and provides relevant bibliography.

Figure 7. The seven tripod clay pithos (a) KT2/94, (b) T66/99 (c)T322/2000, (d)T11/98, (e) T104/99, (f)T121/99, (g)T348/2000 were either mounted directly on the ground, or placed inside distinctive built structures.

over time, exclusively by the senior official of the region, actually existed, reinforcing Sherratt's ideological framework[29] *'that the practice of feasting was, although not a preserve of the elite, something that symbolized their lifestyle'*. Thus, it is my opinion that the same applies for the elite's residence.

In the case of Protogeometric Stamna's population, the tripod pithos and tripod jars that were used, in the discussed researched cemetery (Figure 7), to include the remains of the cremations, the inurned inhumations and their offerings, testify that even when limited, the rationale of utilitarian sequence of objects in life and death exists. The tripod clay pithos vessels found and used as urns[30] (Figure 7 {(a)-(e)}) do not show any significant burning traces in their lower part that could indicate their earlier, intense functional use as opposed to the small T104 vessel (Figure 8) that displays intense burning traces.[31] The whole

---

[29] Fox 2012, 75.
[30] Christakopoulou 2009, 1042.
[31] Christakopoulou 2009, 300, T104. Handmade tripod vase, tightly enclosed by a group of vessels (cups 2, amphoriskos 1, trefoil oinochoe 1, hydria 1, pyxis 1). Few burning residues were found inside. Since, in another perspective, the vase contained only burnt offerings for the dead of

construction of T104 suggests the cremation of a young person, perhaps even an infant, but as only adult cremation is reported, perhaps the fire derived exclusively from accompanying offerings to the two burials found in the neighboring pithos burial T85. In the group of tripods there is also a four-handled amphora T324[32] (Figure 9) whose legs were removed[33] and included the buried residues and not an incinerated dead.[34] The vessel, whose symposium status represented the superior hierarchy, was covered with four layers of eleven vessels and stone pile of clay limestone, sandstone, and conglomerate stones. A special characteristic feature was the limitation of each layer of offerings to a narrow, irregular quadrilateral space defined by two limestone slabs placed vertically and by three irregular stones.

Perhaps the most interesting chapter on the history of the region according to the excavation so far, is the use of bronze cauldrons as funerary urns. The tripod cauldrons are the most important category of banquet vessels, and although their presence to date in the Early Iron Age Stamna, is small, so far, nevertheless it confirms the performance of elite social gatherings that validated the noble birth, strengthened the position of the powerful residents[35] and were included into the valuable assets of their owners.[36] Their re-use as funerary vessels makes them purely emblematic and confirms their position in society even after their death,[37] which would also strengthen their family's position, if their office was hereditary.[38] According to Wright[39] the use of bronze over clay tripod itself, dictated but also implied the exclusion of most of the population and the

---

pithos 85, it must be admitted that the concept of the construction is original as it imitates a burial one.

[32] Christakopoulou 2009, 518-522; 1054; 2016, 75, fig. 11.

[33] This action was probably performed according to the custom of their ritual destruction in order not to be reused Maran 2012, 124-125.

[34] The bones probably belong to a young person, who as such did not belong to the age category of those to be cremated.

[35] For a brief presentation of the elite of the Proto-Geometric period see Mazarakis – Ainian 2009, 20-21; see also Alexandridou 2016, 351-352, with relevant chronology, where the writer summarily refers to the use of copper cauldrons/urns, providing literature on their use as an indicator of the age and gender of the dead, the wealth of their owners and their differentiation in the socio-cultural environment of the era. Regarding the sex of the dead, among others, indicatively mentions that while in Eretria the copper cauldrons contained men and women, in Athens they contained only male burials.

[36] Barrowclough 2014, 14, *'suggesting that it was considered precious or possibly even 'sacred' having mystical associations with smiths, chieftains, warriors and gods'.* Gerloff 2010, 120 (after Barrowclough ibid) argues that *'The size and technical complexity of cauldrons certainly suggests that they were high status objects connected to a ceremonial or ritual function'.*

[37] Whitley 2002, 223-224.

[38] See above, Mazarakis – Ainian 2009, 20.

[39] Wright 2004, n.56.

Figure 8. The small T104 vessel which was used as an urn and was accompanied by six pouring-drinking vessels and a pyxis.

Figure 9. The four-handled amphora T324 (with removed legs), which contained the buried remains of a high ranked dead. Placed vertically on the ground, covered by four clearly distinct layers of offerings and a pile of stones. Probably accompanied the dead of pithos T323.

selective presence of particular people.[40] With regard to the bronze cauldrons, the theoretical background remains the same. Even according to Dabney and Wright,[41] exclusion and limited participation validated their ties with their ancestors, legitimized and strengthened the relations between the participants in the ceremony.

Their use as an integral subject that accompanies every leading figure from time to time in the early Iron Age until the later geometric years is reflected in the geometrical crater *New York 14.130.15* where among other scenes, hoplites surround a tripod cauldron *'...perhaps to portray the type of activities that the deceased had performed in order to display his status or perhaps to emphasize again the association between those of warrior status and feasting events'.*[42] The relationship between the bronze tripod cauldrons and the clay tripod pithos with the ruling class of Stamna, whose countenance is governed by the *attributa* that characterize a worthy warrior, has already been discussed.[43] The same stands for the similarities and more generally the issue involving the origin of the custom and the combined use of the metal urn with the Homeric hero.[44] To the characteristic of this leadership/heroic character, which is supposed to belong to the elite of the elites of the population,[45] the organization of ceremonies including symposiums is also added.

As evidenced by the existing archaeological data and the relevant literature, Stamna is not differentiated, but instead it is included in the social environment of the Iron Age which has been formed in areas where we have representative settlements such as Attica, Eretria, Lefkandi. It becomes apparent, that individual elements such as for example the option between inhumation and cremation of the dead differ locally, more or less, but the basic ideological orientation remains the same. In the emblematic character of the burial structures of Stamna (apsidal with a bench and well type built graves), on the burial tripod vessels that are indicative of symposiums of the high rank and now include cremations (bronze cauldrons incorporating cloth and tripod pithos), on all vessels (types of pouring and drinking) which also indicate symposium as does the presence

---

[40] Borgna 2004, 263.
[41] Dabney and Wright 1990; also see Borgna 2004, 263, stressing once again the dismissive nature of most of the population as *'the occurrence of precious metal vessels suited to drinking appears to confirm that Mycenaean convivial habits favored exclusion rather than cohesion'.*
[42] Fox 2012, 76.
[43] Christakopoulou 2016.
[44] Crielaard 2016, 49, table 1, where a brief chronological list of cremations hosted in metal urns is cited. Referring to prior to the eighth century cremations in metallic urns, he argues that it is a custom predating the Homeric epics, and thus they were considered as a model in their subsequent writing; see also relevant bibliography; also Coldstream 2011, 801.
[45] Crielaard 2016, 55.

of fragments of iron which may be spits, and finally on the whole of the armor found inside them and indicate the military status of the deceased, the finding of fabrics both in a bronze basin and on a tripod bronze cauldron must also be added.[46] It should be taken under consideration that already during the first excavations, a well type built grave T378 (Figure 10), which included cremation in a tripod cauldron covered with cloth, had been discovered. To sum up,[47] these elements are *attributa* to a strong leadership through which the practices and the values of the leaders of the Proto-geometric period are displayed vigorously, where the demonstration of heroic spirit and symposium were distinct actions in the broad spectrum of the life of the population of Stamna, which focused on excellence, success and distinction.

The use of urns of rare and expensive material in a group of graves that may include important members of the Stamna community is also contrasted with the use of handmade vessels. It is likely that the use of handmade urns (Figure 11) declared participation in a higher social class on its own, albeit at a lower level than the dead of the same clan, as it was also assumed from the deposition of hand-made vessels as offerings. The latter concerns members of the community who also participated in banquets and their status would justify their cremation and the encapsulation of their ashes in vessels which were used for small scale banquets, while on the other hand the use of these vessels would also testify and perpetuate the normal day-to-day activity of the locals.[48]

B. Material evidence of consumption: The ceramic dinner sets

Already in LHIIIC period the goblet, which is the prime libation vessel, was abandoned[49] and we have the presence of vessels that incorporate the activities of mixing, drinking and eating.[50] The presence of goblets supported power of the *Anax* and their abolition and the use of different and more common vessels, as mentioned above, symbolized a more admirable relationship and cooperation between the parties, rather than the symbolic imposition of a single person. Since there is no residential testimony in Stamna and therefore no pottery associated with specific places and therefore specific ceremonial events has been found, we cannot identify with certainty specific types of

---

[46] Christakopoulou 2016, 64, n.55.
[47] Dakoronia 2006, 503, argues that it is the combination of elements referring to the typology of graves and the kind of offerings along with their corresponding symbolic meaning, rather than individual items themselves, that lead to the identification of the elite.
[48] For a discussion regarding to handmade pithos shaped vessels and their use in Naxos see Papadopoulou – Zapheiropoulou 1965, 522 and Charalambidou 2008-2009, 62, pl.5g-h; 2011,142, pl.6c.
[49] Hägg 1990, 183· Cavanagh & Mee 1998, 115.
[50] Fox 2012, 61.

16 To Die in Style!

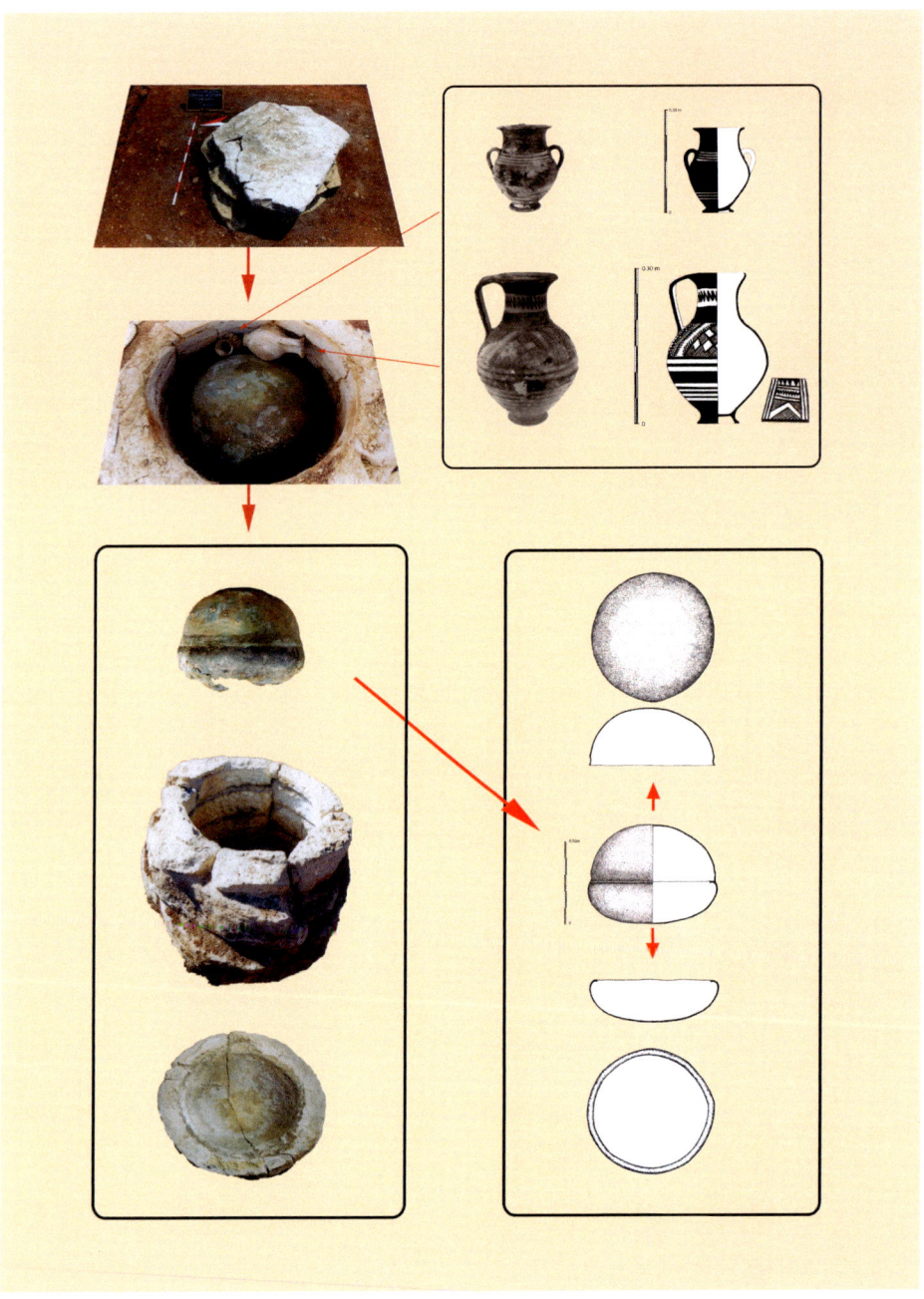

Figure 10. The well type built grave T378, where two bronze cauldrons were included, the first in upright position and the second used as a lid. The cremated remains of the high rank officer were covered by fabric, while the whole process was semantically sealed by the placement of pouring and drinking vessels.

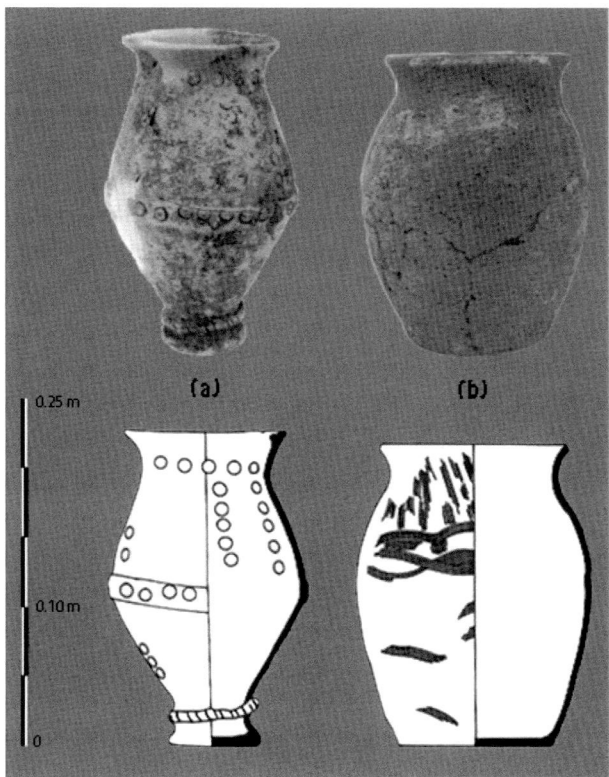

Figure 11. Handmade urns (a) T170/1999 (impressed pottery) and (b) T54/1998 (incised pottery). They form unique examples in the so far excavated and studied cemetery, in terms of their technical construction and also the burial customs themselves.

vessels accompanying burials, with specific rituals of any kind. The data therefore may not be sufficient, the role, however, of the ceramic types found, is distinct through the burial sequence which forms a mixture of articulated parts, summarized in the architecture of the tombs, in the types of offerings and sometimes in their ostentatious placement. As reference to the importance of the architectural types of tombs[51] has already been made, in this chapter we will focus on assessing the typology of vases accompanying their dead.

In the Stamna cemetery the hitherto evidence suggests the use of large tripod vessels as grave jars without possible previous preparatory use,[52] and the simple

---

[51] Christakopoulou 2016.
[52] The latter is justified by the absence of burning traces in its exterior surface and by the absence of a fire near their deposition area. The removal of the three legs from the bronze cauldron T378 could be seen as symbolic, in the sense that in this way they eliminate the possibility of their re-

placement of the vessels within them as a symbolic presence of their formerly symposium use.[53]

This, of course, does not invalidate the assumption that the last meal for large or small-scale feasting rituals took place outside the cemetery,[54] depositing outside or inside the tomb of the deceased either empty pots or vessels filled with liquid offerings, as evidenced by their sealing with skyphos or cups as lids. A similar interpretation could be given to all other graves, regardless of their typology, in which (in particular) a large number of vessels were found.

The vast majority of them consisted of a combination of oinochoae[55] and amphoras, which combine the most representative pots related to pouring and drinking. Classifying the pots by numbers[56] and in the light of a more detailed presentation becomes evident that in the graveyard of Stamna, amphoras, oinochoae and cups in total, form the most populous wheelmade and handmade categories of vessels, which also constitute tight banquet sets in terms of both typology and chronology. As mentioned above, the quantitative superiority of banquet vessels in some tombs is impressive, as for example 29 vessels in Pithos T55/98, 27 vessels in Pithos T13/98, 25 vessels in the Cist Tomb T49/99, 22 vessels in Pithos T38/98, 18 vessels in Pithos T58/99, 17 vessels in the Cist Graves T21/98 and T56/98, 16 vessels in Pithos T1/98 (Table 1), whereas, on the contrary, in the original burial structures their number is extremely limited (see indicative Table 2 defining the types of vessels per grave). More specifically,

---

use, something that reminds us of the destroyed ceremonial sword and spear found in the vaulted tomb Stamna, Christakopoulou 2001, 160-163. Barrowclough 2014, 14, argues that cauldrons could be used as a food production utensil by placing hot stones inside it for water heating, which later would be used in order to boil meat. In this case, burning elements would not be visible in the lower periphery of the metal.

[53] As for the graves of San Montano Węcowski, 2012, 28, refers to sympotic symbolism, and to the use of symbolic vases related to symposium and specifically to *'clear sympotic pattern'* or *'clear sympotic pairs'* (p.29) or *'drinking sets* (p.35)'. He argues (p.24) that: *There is a clear 'default' pattern, which required, in the case of interments equipped with grave goods, the dead to be accompanied in their tombs by at least one oinochoē, i.e. a vessel designed to pour the wine already mixed with water into a cup, and one drinking-cup... The uniformity of this category of 'minimal' grave goods should, in my opinion, be interpreted above all in symbolic terms'.*

[54] As in earlier societies, cf. Cavanagh and Mee 1998, 111. In Lefkandi, a specific space within the Toumba cemetery, where large tripod imprints were found (see Popham et al 1980, 214), was interpreted as a place for the preparation of a funeral banquet and according to the researchers this finding could support the theory that the in situ preparation of food for funeral supper was customary in the cemetery (Unfortunately, the poor quality of the soil does not allow the maintenance of animal bones in order for their scientific analysis to be performed and consequently the theory to be documented, Fox 2012, 82, n.46).

[55] Kourou 1999, 175 argues that vessels such as oinochoae and jugs are useful for liquid offerings, and not obligatory necessary in order to perform convivial ceremonies.

[56] Christakopoulou 2009, 1094.

Tomb Type / Property	Indicative Content in Vases / Correlations of vase groups
PITHOS T55/1998 (Figure 30) I.Kousaridas Christakopoulou – Sotrakou 2009 170, fig. 33-34 pl. 33	**29 vessels** (amphoriskos 20, oinochoae 3, kantharos 1, cup 1, kratiriskos 2 and two unidentified vessels. T55/1 is a handmade urn).
PITHOS T13/1998 (Figure 31) I.Kousaridas Christakopoulou – Sotrakou 2009, 69, fig. 9, pl. 17.	**27 vessels** (outside the pithos: amphoriskos 11, cups 2, oinochoae 6 -of which 5 trefoil-, handmade jug 1, lekythos 1, flasks 2, skyphos 1, triple kernos 1, askos 1, all side by side excluding amphoriskos T13/1 found inside the pithos. The group below, indicative of its use, was found in front of the stomion and consisted of: trefoil oinochoe T13/31, skyphos T13/32, triple kernos T13/33, askos T13/34).
CIST GRAVE T49/1999 (Figure 32) G. Kontomitsos Christakopoulou – Somakou 2009, 239, fig.61, pl.52.	**25 vessels** (identified: flask 1, phiale 1, hydria 1, skyphos 1, triple kernos 1, oinochoae 3, jug 1, cup 2, kratiriskos 1, amphoriskos 2).
PITHOS T38/1998 (Figure 33) I.Kousaridas Christakopoulou – Somakou 2009, 126, fig. 22, pl. 26	**22 vessels** (large handmade amphora 1, trefoil oinochoae 3, jug 1, amphoriskos 15, kantharos 2. It seems that both inside and outside the graves, sets of vessels were grouped according to their type and consequently their use. The first group included the findings T38/1 to T38/18 and the second the amphoriskos type vessels T38/21, 2, 23, 24. In the first group a large handmade amphora, typical sample of liquid storage vessel was accompanied by trefoil oinochoae 3, jug 1, amphoriskos 11 and kantharos 2. All these surrounded the group B at a lower level). In those grouped sets one can easily observe that the vast majority of amphoriskos type vessels is decorated with wavy line patterns. A pair of kantharos T38/8 and T38/13 with rich décor defined by triglyphs and metopes, is also included.
PITHOS T58/1999 (Figure 34) G. Kontomitsos Christakopoulou – Somakou 2009, 261, fig. 65-66, pl.55	**18 vessels** (identified: flask 1, askos 2, amphora 1, amphoriskos 2, oinochoae 5, handmade jug 1, skyphos 1, kanthariskos 2, kratiriskos 1).
CIST GRAVE T21/1998 (Figure 35) I.Kousaridas Christakopoulou – Somakou 2009, 90, fig. 12, pl. 19.	**17 vessels** (they are considered among the most important as a team of pouring and drinking vessels and they were placed with extreme care outside the tomb, lined with their edge lying under the base of the latter and forming a slightly curved line, the two edges of which leaned out, defining the grave. The order was as follows: oinochoae T21/1, amphoriskos T21/8, unidentified T21/7, kratiriskos T21/6, kantharos T21/3, cup T21/4, unidentified T21/5, oinochoe T21/2. Kratiriskos T21/9 was also included in the group although it has been shifted from its original position. Within the cist grave two groups of findings: A. trefoil oinochoe T21/10 together with the cup T21/17, amphoriskos T21/12 13, 14. B. Oinochoe T21/11 among with the cups T21/15,16).
CIST GRAVE T56/1998 (Figure 36) I.Kousaridas Christakopoulou – Somakou 2009, 185, fig. 35, pl. 33	**17 vessels** (oinochoae 6, amphora 1, amphoriskos 9, kantharos 1).
PITHOS T1/1998 (Figure 37) I. Kousaridas Christakopoulou – Somakou 2009, 44, fig. 2, pl. 14.	**16 vessels** (in two superposed layers, of which: oinochoae 2, amphoriskos 12, kantharos 1, kratiriskos 1. Specifically on the SW wall of the pithos, oinochoe T1/3 is accompanied by the amphoriskos type vessels T1/4, 5, 6. Immediately beside the pithos' inner stomion oinochoe T1/7 is accompanied by amphoriskos T1/8 and even its base lies within its stomion. Further and at the level of the shoulder of the pithos, kratiriskos T1/9 was found along with amphoriskos T1/10, while the two-handled amphora T1/11 was found along with amphoriskos T1/12. Kratiriskos T1/16 was accompanied by amphoriskos T1/17, 18, 19, 20, 21).

Table 1. Indicative Content in Vases Correlations of vase groups.

Tomb Type / Property	Related burials / offerings
Apsidal tomb (Figure 1) **S. Mavrommatis** Christakopoulou – Somakou 2009, 35-43, pl.1-13. Christakopoulou 2016, 72, fig.3.	**A. Tripod pithos. Cremation.** Amphoriskos 2 (inside), oinochoe 2 and sherds of unidentified vessels 2 (outside). **B. Two handled amphora. Cremation.** **C. Four handled amphora. Cremation.** Iron sword 1, bronze shield 1, bronze spearhead 1. **D. Inhumation.** Gold hair spirals 2, bronze rings 2, iron rings 2, iron spits fragments (?) 85, clay button 1, bronze leaf-shaped spearhead 1, amphoriskos 1, kantharos 1. **Built bench**: jug 1, kantharos 1, (related either to the inhumation or the cremated dead of the two-handled amphora **B** which is not accompanied by any other findings)
Two handled pithos T11/1998. (Figure 38) **A. Kostadimas** Christakopoulou – Somakou 2009, 222, fig. 8, pl. 16-17.	**Not embedded in a pit Cremation.** Inside the urn: Bronze phiale 1, iron spearhead 1, iron knives 2, a residue of *psimmithion*. Off urn: one vessel.
Built shaft tomb 66 (Figure 39 - Figure 24) **A. Kostadimas** Christakopoulou – Somakou 2009, 416, fig. 69-70, pl. 57-58. Christakopoulou 2016, 72, fig.4.	**Tripod pithos embedded in a well-built shaft grave. Cremation.** Along with the ash sea shells, unidentified vessel sherds and charred wood were collected. Within the shaft: iron spearhead, iron sword, iron pins. Within the tripod pithos: pin fragments? bronze rings 5, bronze hair spiral 1. Beside the tomb and the pithos: trefoil oinochoe 1, clay lid 1.
Built shaft tomb 322 (Figure 40) **Sp. Floros** Christakopoulou – Somakou 2009, 648, fig.192, pl.155-156. Christakopoulou 2016, 73, fig.5.	**Tripod pithos jar in a built structure imitating the well type built shaft grave. Cremation.** Iron spearhead 1, iron knife 1, iron dagger 1, bronze ring 1.
Built shaft tomb 324 (Figure 9) **I. Papadopoulos** Christakopoulou – Somakou 2009, 518, fig.193, pl. 158. Christakopoulou 2016, 75, fig.11.	**Four handled tripod jar with lid. Incineration.** 11 pots in four superimposed layers. *Layer A*. Trefoil oinochoae 3, cup 1. *Layer B*. Oinochoe 2. *Layer C*. Amphoriskos 3. *Layer D*. Amphoriskos 2.
Built shaft tomb 378 (Figure 10) **Pesli** Christakopoulou – Somakou 2009, 714, fig. 216-218, pl. 176-177. Christakopoulou 2016, 73, fig.6.	**Bronze tripod cauldron enclosed in a well like-built shaft grave. Cremation.** Inside the cauldron: iron spearhead 1, iron nail 1, one iron oxidized unidentified object, iron spearhead 1, iron knives 2, iron sword 1, (all wrapped in a cloth), iron pins 2, button 1. Leather (?) covering the interior of the cauldron from side to side. Outside the cauldron/urn: trefoil oinochoe 1, amphoriskos 1.
Cist grave T20/1999 (Figure 41) **Communal property.** Christakopoulou – Somakou 2009, 934, fig. 50, pl.42-43.	**Inhumation.** Inside the grave: large two-handled amphora. Bronze pins 2, Iron and bronze rings.

Table 2. Related burials. Offerings.

Tomb Type / Property	Related burials / offerings
Pithos T63/1998 (Figure 42) I. Kousaridas Christakopoulou – Somakou 2009, 203 fig. 41, pl.36.	**Inhumation.** Inside the grave: large two-handled amphora along with kratiriskos 1, oinochoe 2, amphoriskos 5.
Pithos T133 (Figure 43) A. Koukounas Christakopoulou – Somakou 2009, 981, fig. 96, pl.84.	**Inhumation.** Inside the grave: large two-handled amphora along with unidentified sherds and an iron pin.
Cist grave T227 (Figure 44) Communal property. Christakopoulou – Somakou 2009, 952, fig. 139, pl.121.	**Inhumation.** Inside the grave: large two-handled amphora.
Cist grave T35/1999 (Figure 45) Communal property. Christakopoulou – Somakou 2009, 937, fig. 57, pl.47.	**2 Inhumations A and B + 1 cremation. Outside the grave:** Unidentified vessel 1. Within the grave: large two-handled amphora containing the burnt residues. The inhumated dead were accompanied by: **A.** Jug 1, iron rings 2, bronze bracelet (*psellion*) 1, bronze pin 1, bronze spearhead 1. **B.** bronze fibula 1, bronze pin 1, bronze rings 3, glass bead 1. +1 copper ring that cannot be ascribed accurately to one of the two burials.
Pithos T385 (Figure 46) G. Gkeka Christakopoulou – Somakou 2009, 908, fig.221, p1.130.	**Inhumation.** Inside the grave: large two-handled amphora + pins 3 (?)

Table 2. Related burials. Offerings.

22 TO DIE IN STYLE!

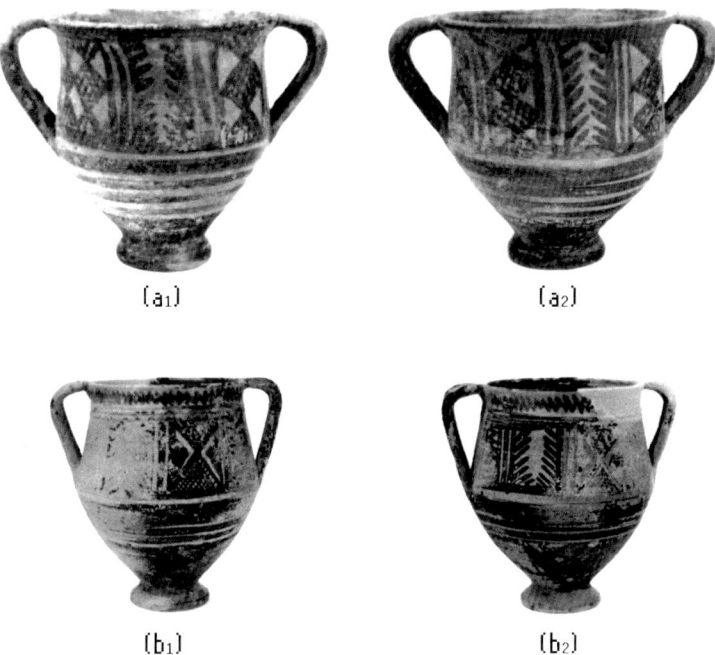

Figure 12. A group of two kantharos: T38/8 (a1- a2) and T38/13 1998(b1- b2), of the same type, bearing the same decoration (triglyfs and metopes) and serving the same use (drinking vessels).

as one perceives from the vessels of the already studied cemetery, the contrast between the graves of the officials and the tombs of the ordinary citizens of Stamna, is remarkable. The average citizen was buried in jars and cist graves accompanied by a large number of vessels in and out of the tomb, while the elite of the society of Stamna was accompanied by a small number or no pots at all, with the exception of T324, comprising of 11 vessels, which were classified into four groups corresponding to the layers, each of which contained either two or three vessels.

With regard to the vases accompanying the dead of Pithos T38/98, it seems that both within and outside the graves there are vessels grouped together in terms of their type and hence of their use. In the grouped sets of T38/98 it is easy to observe that in their overwhelming majority the amphoras are adorned with the wavy lines, while in the group a pair of kantharos is also included (T38/8 and T38/13) with rich decoration defined by triglyphs and metopes (Figure 12). Identical vessels were used in pairs in Crete during the Neopalatial period, in rituals that were related to the hospitality and strengthened personal relationships among communals.[57]

---

[57] Borgna 2004, 259-260.

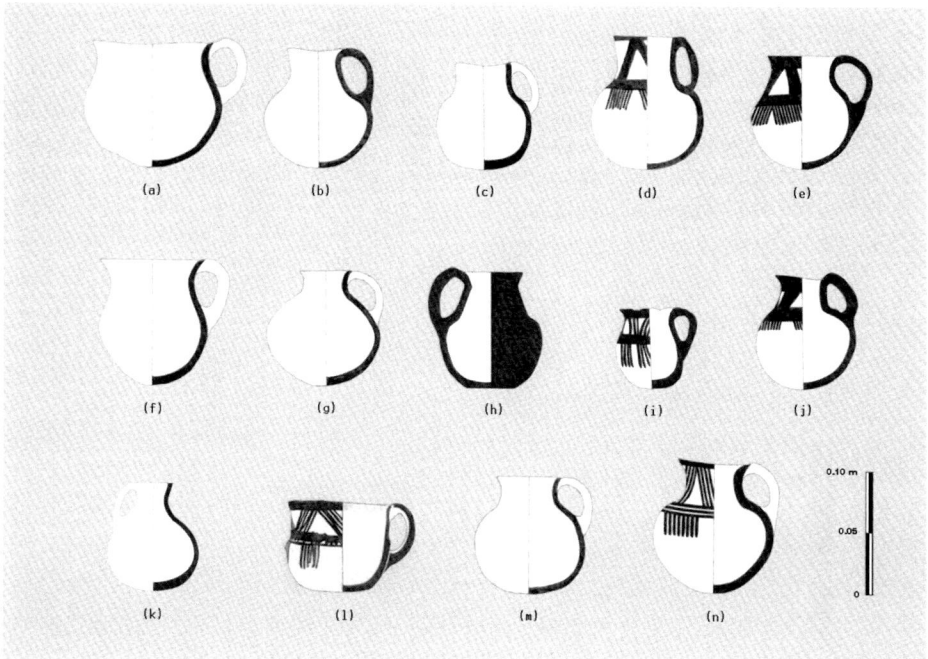

Figure 13. Matt painted pottery (a-n) found in the cemetery of the Stamna region excavated to date. The decoration patterns consist of the same motifs in different variations.

It is obvious that the type of tomb itself was enough to denote the differentiation between the elite and the average citizen. While the latter tried to prove that he qualified- at least - for a symbolic position on the banquet table as a citizen of the Stamna region, the elite itself stands indifferent and simultaneously differentiated itself, as considering the distinction obvious, it was characterized by the symbolic presence of certain types of drinking and pouring vessels.

As there are no residential findings, we cannot be absolute about whether handmade pots[58] found in graves are clearly sub-utilitarian production or were intended purely for exclusive funerary use, except for matt painted pottery respectively (Figure 13), which was found mainly in Thermos and Kato Vassiliki and derive from residential layers. Perhaps it is a pottery that, while once it was purely utilitarian, now its second use is purely funerary. But why are

---

[58] Regarding the handmade/utilitarian ceramics of the Protogeometric period, see also the interdisciplinary dissertation of Jean-Sébastien Gros, *La céramique commune en Grèce centrale au début de l'Âge du Fer (ca. 1100-675 avant J.-C.). Typologies, Production, Circulation, Consommation.* University of Thessaly - Department of History, Archeology and Social Anthropology, Greece and University Paul Valéry – Montpellier III, France. Abstract available in Greek in: https://www.archaiologia.gr/blog/2009/07/29.

there handmade vases also used as offerings for the dead in graves? The logical thing would be to use vessels of a specific typology and elaborate decoration to commemorate the dead in an appropriate manner (in the sense of their selective choice according to typology and decoration). Perhaps, however, the use of handmade vessels with no particularity in terms of their typology, and sometimes even no decoration and which are used either in the preparation of food, or in a daily liquid consumption, declared on their own (or their users would like to declare) a symposium proficiency and hence the high status of the deceased in the local hierarchy.

C. Bronze vessels

As mentioned above and as evidenced by their dimensions, tripod cauldrons are used, among other, for preparing food in major social events involving a significant number of participants. Similarly, tripod clay pithos must be the imitation of bronze cauldrons in terms of their use and hence their symbolic significance. In other words, in the specialized well type built grave constructions of Stamna where a tomb does not contain only a bronze urn but also a clay one, maybe what we should perceive as important for the declaration of the host's status, is not the material (clay/bronze), but the type of the vessel itself.

The existence of the metal vessels in Stamna, renders the burial itself emblematic. But as the economic *dystocia* dominating a population after a movement does not favor the introduction nor the destruction of such a valuable acquisition, with the end of its utilitarian function and the beginning of its use as urns, their replacement by clay tripod pithos would be considered inevitable, as evidenced by both the inclusion of the latter in the original architectural enclosures and their placement as burial offerings which is relevant. It is very important that as a burial custom, the use of large tripod jars and in particular the use of tripod cauldrons which were previously used for the preparation of food in significant events and for high rank citizens, as burial vessels which contain the residues of the cremation of hosts are similar and repeated in the rest of Europe and sometimes associated with witchcraft.[59] The use, therefore, of these oversized metal vessels is directly linked to an ideological content featuring specific social groups, whose identity is determined through the burial sequence. With regard

---

[59] See bronze cauldrons in British Museum from the area of the British Isles and Ireland. http://www.britishmuseum.org/research/research_projects/all_current_projects/chiseldon_cauldrons/cauldrons_and_feasting.aspx. Others were offerings to gods, such as the one found on the River Thames/Battersea, others were of domestic nature, such as in Chiseldon, while they were also used as burial urns such as the one found in Baldock in Hertfordshire. In the latter case, the dead were accompanied by iron firedogs, a common ceremonial/burial process as evidenced by the tomb of Eltinas in Crete, see Rethemiotakis – Egglezou 2010, 176.

to the placement of a bronze cauldron as a warrior's gift, and not as an urn, within a cist grave, the find in Kouvara, Akarnania, should be mentioned as the closest geographic parallel, dated to the Submycenaean period.[60] Furthermore, concerning the organization of ritual banquets that do not relate to burial events as such, but are intended to emphasize the notion of banqueting in terms of a ceremonial event that was taking place in the wider area of Aetolia, reference should be made to Thermon.[61] The latter moreover forms an exceptional center of the sociopolitical authority reflecting the powerfulness of its leaders. The dependence though, of the Stamna society during the early historical times in social/economical/religious level cannot yet be testified by archaeological evidence. However, the association of these societies that functioned at the same time both in Stamna and Thermon cannot be avoided, since making religious ceremonial banquets through funeral ceremonies (Stamna) or also purely for religious purposes (Thermon), is likely to have had similar origins.

Metal vessels were placed in elite tombs. Extremely interesting is the presence within the tomb of a bronze bowl (Figure 14) from which part of the rim is preserved [62] and the finding of a whole bronze bowl,[63] a unique find in Stamna, which suits to a distinguished owner. Both the rarity of finding them in Stamna and elsewhere[64] as well as their use, as judged by the way they were held,[65] indicate their selective use. Clearly the excavation has not been completed but the limited finding of such a luxurious vase in all the tombs that have been excavated to date, can only be seen as indicative of the lifestyle of the owners, whereas in the case of T11/2, the burial belonged to a distinct cluster which included burial layers and peculiar stone constructions. In particular it

---

[60] Stavropoulou – Gatsi, Jung, Mehofer 2012, Christakopoulou 2016, 64. At this point, however, reference should be made to neighboring Ithaca and the 12 dedicated tripods of the 9th - 8th c. found in Polis Cave (or Loizos Cave) and who, along with another found by Loizos, reflect those donated by Alkinoos and the Phaeacians to Odysseus (Odyssey Θ, 387 cc), Kontorli Papadopoulou 469, 2017.

[61] Papapostolou 2009. Fox 2012, 74-75, referring to Thermon and the exceptional building of Megaron B and it's functions, argues that the character of the building and its associated activities differed from all others buildings under study, *'due to regional differences, as Aetolia is the most notherly of all the areas discussed and was by no means progressive during the EIA'*, a theory can now be discussed considering the excavation data that have come to light.

[62] Christakopoulou - Somakou 2009, 222, 1216.

[63] Unpublished excavation of 1992.

[64] For the scarcity of metal vessels in graves of Lefkandi see Crielaard 2006, 288 where the scholar argues that Toumba *'was by far the most prestigious burial ground'*, as -among others- metal vessels with dining equipment were placed exclusively for the high-ranking residents of this particularly residential settlement. For the use of metal vases from the elite in earlier times in Crete, see Borgna 2004, 258.

[65] Crielaard 2013, 142, fig.4 a.b.c.d.

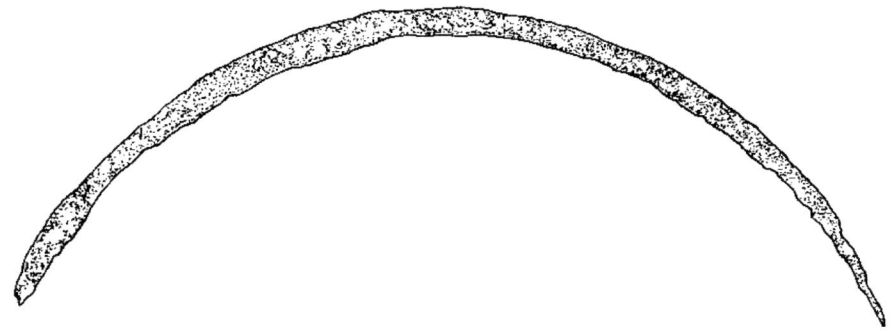

Figure 14. Part of the rim of a deep bronze bowl. Unfortunately, no other part was preserved so as to restore the vase to its potentially original shape.

belonged to a cremated dead, the remains of which were placed in a pithos vessel together with an iron spearhead, two iron knives and a mass of powder.[66]

The existence of these individual findings could be incorporated in one of the already existing theories[67] relating to simple legacy, acquisition of travel, commercial exchange product, (the latter being symbolic indication of the high social status of the deceased having the potential to engage in commercial and naval activities), but also an indication that the population of Stamna was heterogeneous and open to the inclusion of groups and individual residents in its wider environment. This is a theory that we cannot invoke, since no conclusions have been published so far on the alloy and the origin of copper metal objects of Stamna.

Fox,[68] referring to a similar tactic followed over time already from the LHIIIC period in Perati, where two tombs out of the 279 contained metal vessels, and continuing with the Protogeometric Lefkandi, where 11 graves out of 83 also contained metal vessels, speculates that this ceremonial constituted a selective after death offering. Stockhammer[69] referring to the Tiryns metal vases advocates that they should have a direct connection with the ritual banquets during the Post-Palatial period, and thus were buried in graves with this attribute, a theory that also responds to neighboring Achaia and more particularly in Spaliareika

---

[66] Christakopoulou - Somakou 222, fig.8, pl. 16-17.
[67] Fox 2012, 77.
[68] Fox 2012, 77. Iakovides 1980, 99. Popham & Lemos 1996.
[69] Stockhammer 2008, 320–325; 2009.

at Lousika, where the use of a bronze kalathos, probably as a cinerary urn, is testified.[70]

In Stamna, the limited finding of metal vases in the under-examination cemetery may also indicate the distinct origin and position of the deceased host among a group of dead, acquiring a clearly leading role in a society manipulated through symposium rituals. According to Wright[71] in cosmic life, the process of symposium, with the typical that it implies, in itself separates the host from the guest and distinguishes the social position of the participants. Furthermore, the use of certain objects, such as a tripod (or no tripod), cauldrons and tripod clay pithos in Protogeometric Stamna, that once supposedly were used for communal or ritual feastings, is perfectly emblematic and identified with a specific social group.[72] Similarly, in the case of Cyprus, Knapp[73] reports that bronze tripod cauldrons and bronze tripod vases *'were true masterpieces of bronze casting'* and that *'were employed by Cypriote elites to amplify their social position'*. These include bronze tripod bases as well as accompanying objects testifying to banqueting, such as spits and firedogs.[74]

Summarizing, at this point it should be emphasized that especially the combination of the ceremonial banquet with metal tripod vessels, and sophisticated architectural structures, leads us to a formulation of interpretations, at least at the level of assumption, regarding the issues of origin and communication.[75] We should emphasize that, for metal objects, a typical *ante quem* dating is based on related offerings and specifically on ceramics, while, in reality, the time of their construction is not precisely defined, a fact that when it can occur in actual terms via the use of the specialized study of the alloy, it will also reveal the duration of their use.

D. *Complementary feasting equipment: Spits, Hooks and Knives*

If we accept the identification of iron debris in the monumental apsidal tomb of Stamna as multiple fragments of spits (Figure 2), we must, among all other things, wonder about the origin of the custom in the region. The uniqueness of

---

[70] Kaskantiri 2017, 269. see also n.351.
[71] Wright 2004, 134.
[72] For the meaning of the term *emblematic* and especially the significance of the *emblemic display* in order to explain the creation and confirmation of a social identity see Wright 2004, 135; Wiessner 1983, 257-258.
[73] Knapp 1986, 66-69, 77-84; 2006, 54-59, in Maran 2012, 122, with relevant bibliography.
[74] Maran relies on the presence of all these to prove that their discovery reveals cultural relationships, as they appear in elite contexts from Etruria in the West, to Cyprus in the East. See, Maran 2012, 122, with corresponding bibliography.
[75] Christakopoulou 2016.

their discovery as the previously published ensembles have not yielded similar objects, and on the other hand, the identification of the particular burial with a prominent member of the elite, an identification that is intensified by the finding of the spits, differentiates the tomb as a whole in relation to those found in other clusters including built tombs.[76]

In the opinion of the author, it is not worthwhile proceeding to a discussion of which cluster of tombs belonged to the elite of the elites in the wider area of Stamna. As it has already been noted, the population may have been multidimensional in many aspects and perhaps it constituted a mixture of cultural elements encountered in this area, or a mixture collaborating even before settling, and through the typology of the graves of their distinguished members they were thus differentiated.[77] In result, the presence of the spits in the built tomb of Stamna adds another element concerning the puzzle of the origin of the custom referring to a population inhabiting this specific region during the early historical times.[78]

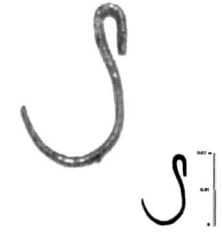

Figure 15. Bronze hook T88/12 1999.

The finding of hooks T51/2 98 (iron) and T88/12 99 (Figure 15) (bronze), also denotes the ideology of the persons concerned, that is people who wish to associate the deceased with a process involving either the pursuit of food and thus their professional status (fishermen), or simply the act of eating. The hooks were found within two graves (T51)[79] (T88)[80] of the Late Protogeometric period from which the dead of the first burial was accompanied by an amphoriskos and an unidentified iron object, while the dead of the second burial (Figure 16) was accompanied by a variety of vessels such as: trefoil jug, cup, kantharos, tripod bowl with missing legs and jewelry consisting of bronze fibulae, arched and foliate bronze bracelets rings, beads, a bronze button and a sea-shell.

---

[76] Christakopoulou 2016.
[77] Christakopoulou 2016.
[78] See Ruiz Galvez - Galan 2012, 43-44; 2012, 50 with relevant bibliography. According to the argumentation of the article, quoting among other that: *'cooking and eating is more than a biological act, it is primarily a socially and culturally constructed behavior'* Steel 2004, 281-282. According the authors the origin of the fashion of roasted meat can be soever sought in the Levant.
[79] Christakopoulou - Somakou 2009, 165, pl. 32.
[80] Christakopoulou - Somakou 2009, 306, pl. 66.

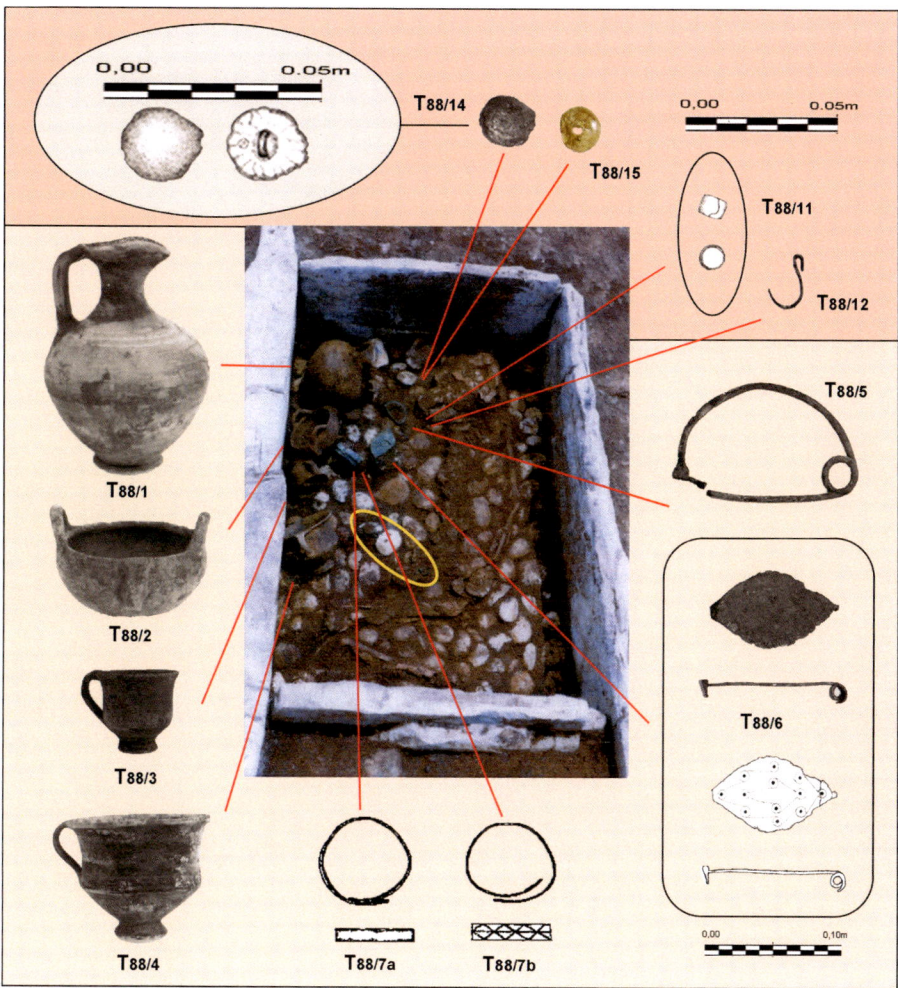

Figure 16. Cist grave 188/1999. An inhumation was found placed in 'foetal' position with the head facing east. Representative drinking and eating type vessels accompanied the dead. Unfortunately, no photos or drawings of the small objects (three rings (T88 8, 9,10 and a glass bead T88/15) were found in the original photo archive but the location of the bronze rings (T88/8,10) worn by the dead is clearly visible in the yellow circle.

Their presence here, not being connected with cauldrons or other cooking pots, must be purely symbolic, a theory that becomes stronger in the tomb T88 with the presence of a clay tripod bowl, which was deposited without the legs and perhaps imitated the large burial ash tripod vases, bronze or not, used in the cemeteries of Stamna. It should be noted that the cist grave T51 belonged to I. Kousaridas plot, with successive burial layers and included significant burials and stone constructions for religious use.[81] Tomb 88 belonged to G. Kontomitsos plot which included in total rich burial offerings, although it typologically lacked all the sophisticated types of tombs already studied,[82] except perhaps the Pithos T85 who was accompanied externally by the tripod cooking vessel T104[83] (Figure 8).

The existence of tripod vessels of any form in the specific clusters, even as a sample, as in the case of the cluster of G. Kontomitsos, indicates the importance that the participation in a banquet event acquired for the corresponding population. In the case of T85 and T104, the deceased may not have occupied an office justifying his participation, but his relatives wanted to grant him this right *post mortem* with the symbolic placement of the small utensil and the household equipment that fulfilled its symbolic character, without though offending the deceased officers who were entitled to it, and who were placed in the shaft well like structures with the tripod pithos and the cauldrons already mentioned.[84]

By the same logic, the deposit of the hooks in these clusters is considered as a small symbolic gesture referring though to social networks of large-scale in terms of evaluation, and apparently without affecting the rights acquired by the privileged class.

The existence of knives either accompanying other weapons, either they were deposited on their own, is also noteworthy [85] (Figure 17). Isolating the instances where they constituted unique offerings in this category (weapons), and since in almost all cases they were joint offerings along with drinking and pouring vessels, the fact of their existence suggests the preference of their use as cutting tools, in some cases exclusively, confirming Catling's view,[86] with regard to the iron knives in Lefkandi. The combination of knives with pouring and drinking vessels also increase the willingness of the close to the deceased persons concerned, to emphasize the participation of the departed in banquet events.

---

[81] Indicatively see, Christakopoulou 2009, T53, pl.32. T50 - T50A, pl. 31.
[82] Christakopoulou 2016.
[83] Christakopoulou - Somakou 2009, 300, fig. 86, pl. 74.
[84] Christakopoulou 2016, see the monumental apsidal tomb 72, fig. 3. T66 99, 72, fig.4. T322 99, 73, fig.5. T378 99, 73, fig. 6. T324 99, 75, fig.11.
[85] Christakopoulou - Somakou 2009, 1248.
[86] Lefkandi I, 257-258.

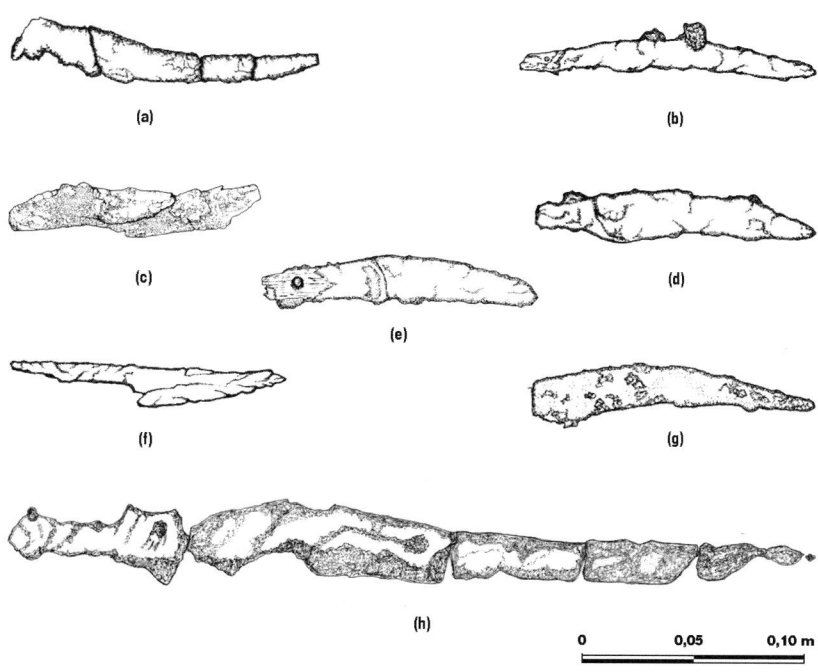

Figure 17. A total of 52 iron knives were found, separated into offensive or cutting tools, depending on the co-findings. Knives (a) T148/7, (b) T91/10 99, (c) T335/9, (d) T363/13 00, (e) T3/ΔM2 98, (f) T56/29 98, (g) T3/ΔM1 98, (h) T38/31 98 are the most representative examples of the category whose participation in graves enhances the availability of the family and close persons to emphasize the participation of the deceased in symposium events. (regarding to the shape and size of (h), this could also be included in the category of daggers).

Fare thee well. The Stamna Timeless Farewell

We are in a transitional period where the population has settled in a new region, and tries to maintain its identity through daily rituals, even via the ones associated with their definitive departure from the world of the living. Those who dominate are trying through a religious standard of 'greeting farewell' to the dead, to strengthen and consolidate their economic and political privileges following tactics and practices to legitimize a hierarchy, as this seems to have been formed after the fall of the Palaces.[87] The settlement of different population

---

[87] For the transfer of power from *anaktes* to *basileis*, the origin of the latter, and the manner in which the symposium operated in this new environment see Fox 2012, 60 with relevant bibliography. Also, Palaima 1995, 124-125 and Dickinson 2006, 60-61. For the theory of the evolution of the lord/rulers of the LHIIIC period to the basileis of the Early Iron Age using as a

groups in the Stamna region imposed on its own the need to establish this hierarchy in the form of a series of ceremonies related to ritual banquets, and the cremation of selected dead from the one side in combination to the existence of tripod vessels used for ritual gatherings in the form of banqueting/feastings on the other, indicates the symbolic significance of this ritual, which is goes back to the Mycenaean times.[88] In the case of Stamna, communal or ritual feastings may also have been carried out among the elites of the different communities in order to prevail a custom already known from the Mycenaean times between the central authority and the regional centers.[89] In other words, the battle for supremacy was about the predominance of a community center, meaning of a central settlement over other smaller that surrounded it.

Stamna's elite, copies the prerequisites defining the status of the elites of the Mycenaean times, which is characterized by participating in hunting (as hunters/gatherers), feasting[90] *(communal and ritual)* and warfare. Their parallel combination incorporated in distinctive funerary architectural constructions (apsidal, well type shaft graves, and other distinctive ones),[91] outlines the sovereign status of the elite, at the same time defines in a notional way the relations between the ruler (i.e those included into the grave) and its subordinates (i.e. all the others who have been buried around him),[92] seeking as a final purpose the hereditary sovereignty[93] of that group (Figure 18). This is a

---

case study the region of Achaia, see Kaskantiri 2017, 434, n.1585.

[88] Maran 2012, 125, where also the relevant literature on the finding of spits and firedogs is appended.

[89] Dabney, Halstead, Thomas 2004, 214. See also n. 40 on De Fidio's 2001, 23-24 argument, regarding the Mycenaean ritual. Livieratou 2011, using as a case study the Argolid Plain and East Phocis efficiently displayed transitional elements related to ritual dining from the Mycenaean period to the Early Iron Age, while arguing about Asine (2001, 51) she quotes that *'...drinking and dining, as well as libation, appear to be involved in cult in both periods'* but with variations as the result of social changes.

[90] Fox 2012, 16 refers to feasting as to an *elite ' package', adopted or at least expressed visually from the end of the MH period'*. See also p.75 where she analyzes this *'ritual package'* reviewing data from the Mycenean era to the Early Iron Age.

[91] Christakopoulou 2016 (outside the modern Greek state area)

[92] At this point it must be emphasized that graves presenting all these particular features are located among the tombs of the same cluster to which they belong, and not at a more distant or prominent position, so as to accentuate the capacity of the dead in this manner as well. This forms an obviously important parameter highlighting the leading status of the deceased as Mazarakis Ainian 2009, 24 points out that: *'The building itself with its monumentality forms a reflection of a leading society, where the leader wants to proclaim his right to rule'*. For the status of the 'prominent' of the residents of the Iron Age in Lefkandi, Toumba and Kavousi, Vronda and how this is reflected through the locality of the houses around his exceptional residence see Whitley 1991, 348 onwards.

[93] See Criellard 2006, 272.

procedural ritual that did not arise suddenly, and it has its origins in a long term established tradition of the population.

Hagg's association,[94] with regard to the bronze houseware found in Tiryns (cauldrons firedogs, cutting knives), with the *central hearth* forming an integral part of the Mycenaean residence, seems to be well founded. The *Hearth* is a basic architectural element and focal point of the daily life both in a simple house and in a megaron, and it also forms the family gathering place, where the concentration of foreign visitors is ideologically interpreted as an introduction process in terms of an 'opening' of the domestic cycle from where the visitors can be accepted in the family itself. Among others, it symbolizes the stability and permanence and beyond the religious/social symbolism it represents the center of the political military community.[95]

To the question of whether Stamna's cauldrons were previously usable, no response can be given before their study is conducted. Their large dimension clearly indicates the preparation of large quantities of food for consumption, and even the preparation and storage of extremely large amounts of liquid content. However, the absence of handles does not increase the chances of using them, as it is self-evident that for their transportation to and from the fire the handles are necessary. It should be noted that the bronze cauldron T378 used for the deposit of the bones of the cremated dead and his grave offerings, which were fully covered by fabric, did not bear any handles and was found lacking the legs.[96]

At this point reference should be made to the tripod cauldrons found at the Tripod's Tomb House in Mycenae[97] as they formed part of the cover of a pit grave, which included a dead deposited with twenty bronze double axes and

---

[94] Hagg 1994

[95] Maran – Stavrianopoulou 2007, 287, citing the relevant literature on the ideology that associates the Mycenaean king as supernatural being to the *Estia/Hearth*, which symbolizes the center of the kingdom of which he is the ultimate defender. In continuation, reference is made to the tempting view of Wright 1994, 57-58, who attempted to specify the character of this ideology by pointing to the close link between throne and hearth, from which he inferred that the hearth symbolized the centre of the state and that the Anax sitting on the throne acted as the lord and protector of this fire. The symbolic importance of Hearth is recognized internationally as the later chronological Type Colchester cauldron was found on the site of the Celtic King Cunobellinus' capital Camulodunum, carefully buried in a pit nearby *'burnt clay patch in a squarish hollow'* which was probably a Hearth *'suggesting that it was considered precious, or possibly even ́sacred, having mystical associations with smiths, chieftains, warriors and gods'*, Barrowclough 2014, 14, with relevant bibliography.

[96] Maran 2012, 124-125, referring to the treasure of Tiryns, argues that the removal of the foot from the copper cauldron was deliberate so as not to be used again after this ritual.

[97] Onasoglou 1995.

Figure 18. The position of the arched tomb (Figure 1) compared with the rest belonging to the same cluster. The burials (pithos burials, handmade pots and cist graves that included child burials), were found accumulated in the central part of the plot and their small number indicates that this cluster hosted exclusively the dead people of the prominent family of the settlement (sketch of the author based on archaeological records).

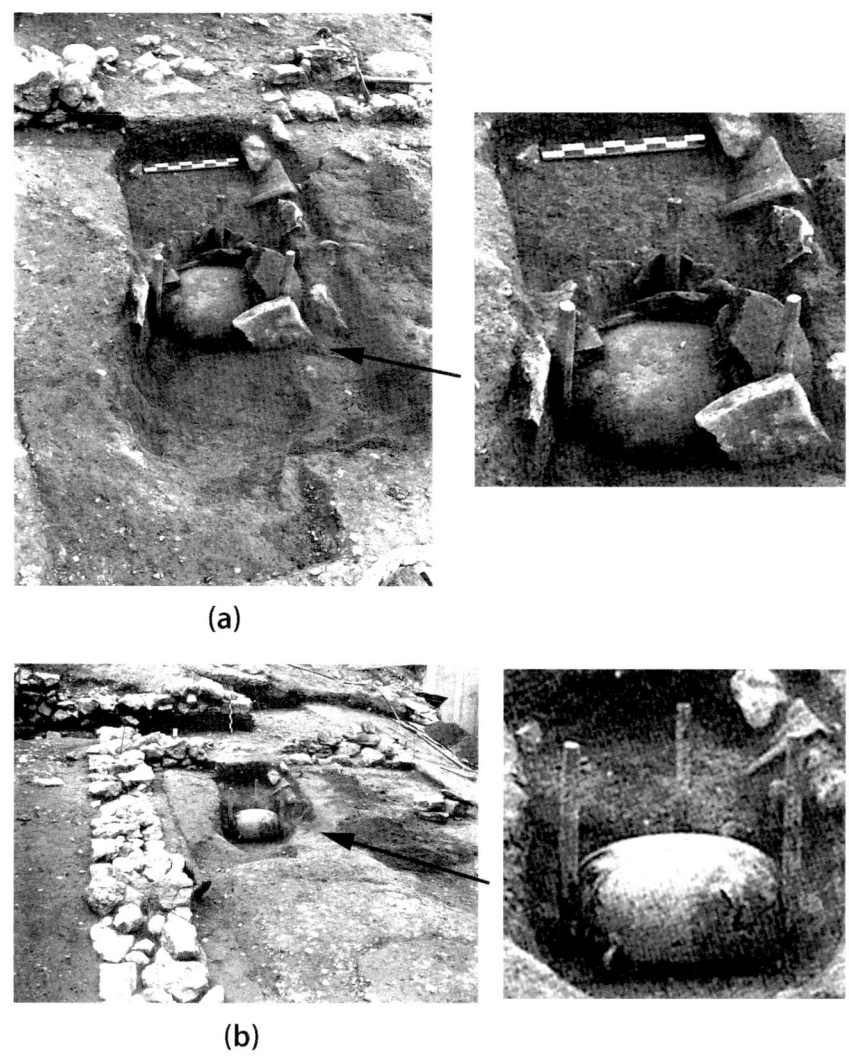

Figure 19. (a) - (b). The cauldron in situ with details (photo archive of The Archaeological Society Foundation. Artemis A. Onasoglou 1995. Η Οικία του Τάφου των Τριπόδων στις Μυκήνες, pl.7a and pl.8a.)

a bronze wedge tool. The cauldrons, one of which was dismembered by the excavation work, and the other one found intact and positioned upside down with the legs protruding (Figure 19), according to A. Onasoglou, reproduce only Mycenaean characteristics and date the burial along with the co-findings between the early LHIIIC and before the start of the Protogeometric period. The concept for the use of bronze cauldrons, which were clearly rare, luxurious and therefore valuable items, shows similarities regarding the burial customs and possessions, deriving from an earlier than the protogeometric era period, when the need to signify the dead as prominent, required the cancelling of the use of the metal cauldrons as household equipment thus rendering them to obsolete objects.

If we consider the burial ritual vessels of Stamna not as separate objects that were used by the elite of the era and treat them as integral elements of a defined space with symbolic significance and social implications,[98] a ritual custom dated back to the Mycenaean era and executed until later times, we recognize a diachronic cultural behavior, which surpasses the narrow regional boundaries of the studied area.

Feasting and Dying in a *lebes*; an institutional innovation with an international appeal

The recognition of symposium processes globally[99] enhances this particular process as a ceremonial ritual, which according to Ruiz Galvez - Galan was introduced in Central and Western Europe during the exchange trade of the Mycenaeans with Italy, and the importance of which is widely accepted, disregarding cultural backgrounds and geographical sections. Barrowclough,[100] among other things, indicates a relative literature of scholars who reduce the origin of cauldrons in Britain from the eastern Mediterranean and the Aegean, as opposed to others that are oriented towards a more northern origin. Gerloff[101] similarly connects the appearance of cauldrons in the UK with movements that took place between the 13th and 12th century, following a *dromos* (course) through the Danube, Central Europe and France. Arnold[102] also reports that in Germany, despite the fact that excavation data exists (feasting equipment implying the involvement of cauldrons), which testifies feasting in the Late Neolithic as well as in the Bronze Age, however the peak of symposium as a field of political action between 600-450 BC (late Hallstatt period), is due to the Greek tradition, and occurred after the colonization of Marseille by the Greeks at the mouth of the Rhöne.

---

[98] See Maran 2012, 130. For the space symbolism in ancient Greece see F. Schwarz *Η Νέα Ανθρωπολογία*, 1991; Vernant, J.P. *Μύθος και σκέψη στην αρχαία Ελλάδα*, 1989.
[99] See Ruiz Galvez - Galan 2012, 48-49, where the relevant literature on Central and Western Europe is appended, along with the dating of the cauldrons found between 1390-1120 BC. See also Joy Jody, *'Fire burn and cauldron bubble' Iron Age and Early Roman cauldrons of Britain and Ireland*, available at:
(https://www.repository.cam.ac.uk/bitstream/handle/1810/246295/OA2044_Joycauldronsfinal.pdf?sequence=1)
[100] Barrowclough 2014, 1-17.
[101] Gerloff 1986, 107.
[102] Arnold 2001, 16.

Despite the geographical distances and the chronology of the international findings,[103] the fact that attracts the attention is not only the use of cauldrons for preparation of food from numerous consumers, but the importance of their use, which is framed by the basic principles of social protection of the indefeasible rights of a 'supranational' elite, summarized in exercising control in each socio - economic system. At this point it should be stressed that *'farewell'* with the particular use of tripod cauldrons implied a ritual related to bravery, as their use was exclusively intended for rituals that took place at particular ceremonies with specific recipients. It is noteworthy that in the *homeric epics* small or large in scale symposiums are recorded as a process that is repeated by Homeric heroes in any occasion, and moreover establishes their own status as such.[104]

It is therefore obvious that the message resulting from the use of ritual tripod cauldrons is indisputable and non-negotiable: superiority of their dead owners to those who are not directly involved in this process.

Symposium, Religion and Cult portrayed through successive layers of burials, (semi) circular constructions and pyres

a. Successive layers of burials. Excavations indicate that the site of Kefalovriso, selected from the beginning as a burial place for the elite residents of Stamna, included at least four burial layers,[105] above which laid the remains of semicircular stone constructions, which in turn were covered with earth and stone piles, as deposits of rushing torrents. Stone structures are mentioned in Kymi, Eretria, Oropos and elsewhere[106] and they are associated with ritual burial procedures according to Crielaard,[107] being not only connected with chthonic cults and worship of the dead and of the ancestors, but also concerning ritual offerings including drinking and eating during a post mortem reception, that according to Antonaccio,[108] was customary from the 10th to 7th century. The strict use of this specific space[109] with successive layers of burials was imposed by the

---

[103] See Barrowclough 2014, 1-17, with the respective bibliography.
[104] Sherratt 2004, 301, on the subject of feasting: '*It is clearly not only an activity of Homeric heroes, but also one that helps demonstrate that they are indeed heroes*'. She 2004, 302 also states that '*Feasting is ubiquitous and constant – it is what Homeric heroes do in company at every opportunity*'.
[105] As an additional way among those mentioned by Crielaard for the veneration of ' *the powerful dead*', Crielaard 2007, 181.
[106] See Crielaard 2007, 177. Also n. 48, 49, 50. Clear reference to a circular construction is made for Kymi, while Kourouniotis at '*Αγγεία Ερετρίας*', 3-4: with regard to the West Gate makes the following reference: '*μέγας σωρός ογκωδῶν λίθων ισχυρῶς κεκαυμένων*'.
[107] Ibid.
[108] Antonaccio 1995, 199-207; 249-250; 256, after Crielaard 2007, 177, n.50.
[109] Pappi 2014, 189, reports that the use of the same burial clusters in Argos, during the Geometric

need to maintain the existing institutions, in order to ensure a society with a structured state framework and with respect to its ideals. The integration of a resident in this cluster perpetuated the status and secured the rights of the citizens of Stamna.

b. (Semi) circular constructions. (Semi) circular stone structures were found in three different plots in Stamna, of which two are adjacent to the position Stathmos, Kefalovryso, (Kousarida's /Kostadima's properties)[110] and the third one is located in Tragana, east of the section of the cemetery and near the site where the large arched tomb was excavated. It needs to be noted that all stone structures were associated only with graves, since there is no evidence to date from recent excavations suggesting a residential facility. Specifically, in the Kostadima's plot these (semi) circular shaped structures were defined by irregularly carved boulders, of medium size, placed in two rows, creating in result a sense of a narrow aisle (Figure 20). Unfortunately, the cultivation of the earth with agricultural machinery has destroyed the course of the constructions, and therefore we do not have a complete knowledge of their sequence. However, in places where they survived, the investigation inside them yielded important findings related to anthropomorphic and zoomorphic figurine fragments suggesting ritual worship.[111] Although the stone constructions in Kousarida's plot did not survive in the form found in the neighboring property, however it is obvious that it stretched throughout both properties and they were intended for worship ceremonies for all the dead that were included in that cluster. The dead, regardless of the burial layer, were entitled to participate in the same worship process, a fact reflecting the indissoluble cohesion of the specific population, while being particularly revealing about their social position among the other groups, contributing as such to the interpretative approach of the religious and 'urban' field. As mentioned above, similar stone constructions were located east of the arched tomb and define child burials in handmade pots.

c. Pyres. Regarding the extent of the cemetery, the pyres detected and identified with relative safety are scarce (24)[112] (Table 3). Their remnants testify the burning of offerings, in honor of the loved ones, while the pyres were

---

period constitutes the main burial practice and declares *'emphasis on kinship, continuity and then reference to the past'*. Also, that the re-use of the same tombs, which is not common in Stamna, but also the use of heirlooms *'emphasize the traditional character of Argos, which insists on strengthening links with ancestors and enhance the power and prestige of powerful family members'*.

[110] Unfortunately, the excavation in this property was not completed and the plots were not thoroughly researched, but it is estimated that the successive burial layers encountered on the Kousarida property are also extended in Kostadimas.

[111] Christakopoulou, forthcoming.

[112] For a particularly expressive analysis of the importance of fire and how it rules the relationship between the living /dead and the divinities see above n.12.

Figure 20. (a) Photo of the structures in Kostadima's plot. (b) Detail of the structures where an aisle between the two "walls" is visible. (c) Google earth photo including a drawing of the construction within the property, based on the photos included in the author's PhD dissertation (the drawing is made by Maria Golfinopoulou and the author). This kind of individual areas with such constructions were also found on Kousarida's plot, but unfortunately the use of machinery in previous years has destroyed their course at a level that their use could not become apparent at the beginning of the excavation. On the contrary, on Kostadima's plot the course of the construction is more distinct.

mostly not particularly intensive, excluding those that had taken place within curved quadrangular pits, lined with stones, where the burning traces were intense and in some cases the fire had eroded the offerings.[113] Their diameter did not exceed 1.65 m, they were carried out on the ground, in shallow but also in deeper pits, and their outline was clear and defined with the help of greater or lesser accumulation of stones, depending on the size of the pyre, limiting

---

[113] Pyre 7/T152, Christakopoulou 2009, 986.

thus its intensity and at the same time sealing it. The pyres that accompanied the tombs were either adjacent to the tombs or just above them.[114]

According to Table 3, they are classified into four categories: the first includes the ones that, although applied to specific dead they cannot be safely associated. The second category provides a secure link between them, while the third concerns pyres belonging to ceremonial spaces and their implementation is associated with a wide network of ceremonial functions and has a collective character.[115] The fourth category is most likely related to cremations directly associated with the adjacent graves and as the excavation indicates, they were performed in situ.

In the *first category*, in all of the studied burial clusters stands out once again the one of the Kousarida's property. The identification of eight of these in the particular area, at close distances and depths, despite the fact that they cannot be accurately correlated with specific burials, however reveals a typical and repetitive ritual in the form of *enagismos* (Figure 21). The case of Pyre 7[116] of the 1998 excavation period (Figure 22), where a handmade vessel contained cremated remains, possibly of a young person, needs to be addressed differently. The vase was fractured in the burnt soil and a small quantity of sherds, an iron spearhead and an unidentified copper mass were collected.[117] The type of vessel shows its former status in domestic use and perhaps its participation in the cremation ceremony.

Representative pyres of the *second category* are: Pyre 12[118] (Figure 23), four sided in shape, full of sherds, charred material, animal bones and charcoal, which was associated with the well type built grave which encapsulated the bronze cauldron T378, although it was recovered at a higher level of 0.50m. Similar were the materials of the Pyre A T66[119] (Figure 24), which was associated with a tripod pithos in a well type built tomb. Directly associated with the last burial in the Stamna apsidal tomb[120] were the burning residues found on the submerged limestone slabs, where in ash layer (diameter 1m / th.0.40m) two oinochoae were included, which is the primary type of pouring vessels (Figure 25).

---

[114] Take for example the pyres on Kousarida's plot pl.21.
[115] As mentioned above in the text for the interpretation of the (semi)circular constructions in Kousarida's cluster, pl.20.
[116] Christakopoulou 2009, 169.
[117] Christakopoulou 2009, 1088.
[118] Christakopoulou 2009, 711.714.
[119] Christakopoulou 2009, 422.
[120] Christakopoulou 2009, 35.

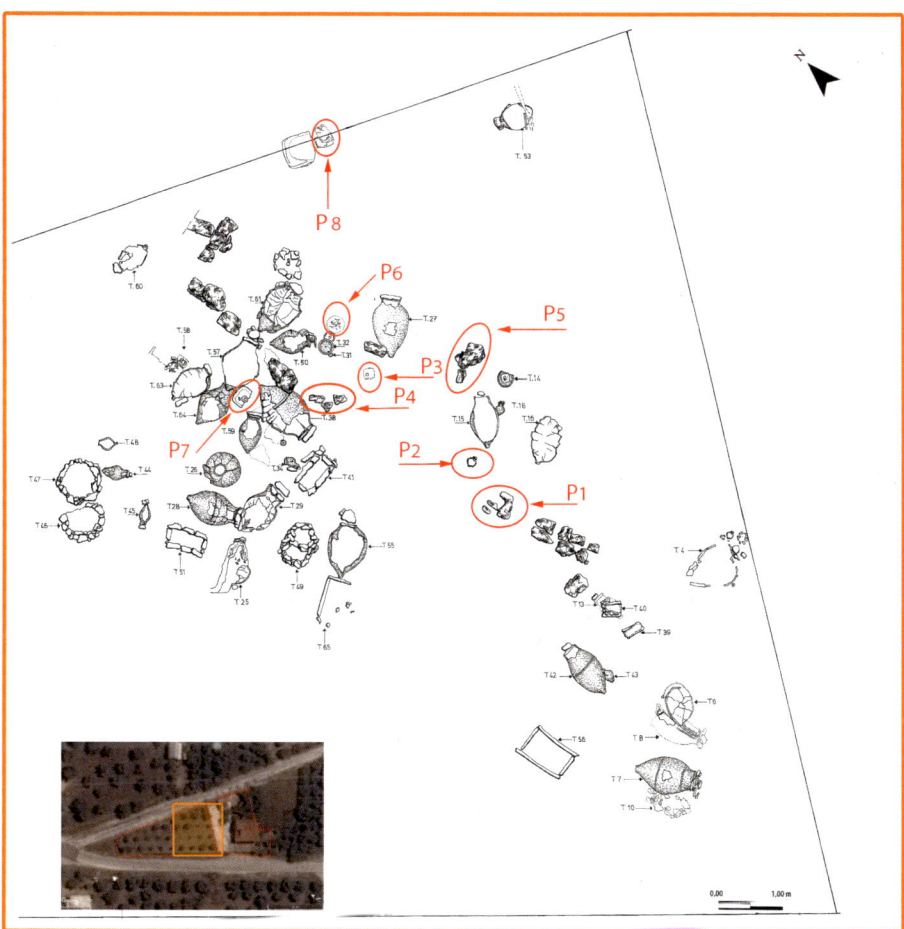

Figure 21. Excavation period 1998. Tombs and pyres on Kousarida's plot. The original plan of ST Ephorate of Prehistoric and Classical Antiquities, dealing with the graves studied to date and designed by Dimitropoulou Ioanna and Katsarkli Georgia has been modified by the author.

Property	Pyres	Delineation / Correlation
S.Mavrommati/ classification 2, Christakopoulou – Somakou 2009, 36.	Apsidal tomb	1X.40. Associated with the last burial in the tomb in a clay tripod pithos. It included two trefoil oinochoe and sherds of at least two closed vessels.
I.Kousarida/ classification 1, Christakopoulou – Somakou 2009, 115.	Pyre 1 (1998)	0.73X1.30X0.65. Burnt soil and sherds. Strongly disturbed embankment.
I.Kousarida/ classification 1, Christakopoulou – Somakou 2009, 116.	Pyre 2 (1998)	diam.=1X0.10. Circular shape. Burnt soil and sherds.
I.Kousarida/ classification 1, Christakopoulou – Somakou 2009, 117.	Pyre 3 (1998)	0.55X0.55. Quadrilateral, burnt soil, charred bones, base of incandescent vessel.
I.Kousarida/ classification 1, Christakopoulou – Somakou 2009, 121.	Pyre 4 (1998)	1.65X1.55. Found at the same depth with Pyres 1, 2, 3. Burnt soil and sherds.
I.Kousarida/ classification 1, Christakopoulou – Somakou 2009, 211.	Pyre 5 (1998)	1.20X0.70. Burnt soil. An iron lamina was collected.
I.Kousarida/ classification 1	Pyre 6 (1998)	(without any references)
I.Kousarida/ classification 1, Christakopoulou – Somakou 2009, 169.	Pyre 7 (1998)	Urn T54, 1m NE of Pyre 6. Found crushed within residues of burning that included burnt clay and sherds. Primarily included the remains of the pyre, which after breakage they were scattered in a semicircular place 0.70X0.70X0.20. Its burnt surfaces indicate that it was also included in the fire. Sherds, a small iron spearhead, and a copper unidentified mass were collected. Probably the vase was included in the remnants of a funeral feast fire and its surfaces were already burned as a result of its utilitarian use.
I.Kousarida/ classification 1, Christakopoulou – Somakou 2009, 202.	Pyre 8 (1998)	1.10X0.90. Irregular quadrilateral shape. Scattered sherds, two bronze rings.
Kostadima/ classification 3, Christakopoulou – Somakou 2009, 219.	Pyre A (1999)	0.45X0.65X0.07. Elliptical shape. It was defined by limestones and sandstone. Soil and charcoal.
Kostadima/ classification 3, Christakopoulou – Somakou 2009, 220.	Pyre B (1999)	Circular shape. Thin layer of burnt soil.
Kostadima/ classification 3, Christakopoulou – Somakou 2009, 221.	Pyre C (1999)	0.90X0.45X0.20. Irregular shape. Burned soil, charcoal, sherds.
Kostadima/ classification 2, Christakopoulou – Somakou 2009, 422.	Pyre A/T66	Related to the well type shaft grave T66 and contained ash, burned bones and burnt wood.
G.Kontomitsos/ classification 2, Christakopoulou – Somakou 2009, 278.	Pyre A/T75 (1999)	1.19X0.20. Ashes. Associated with the dead of pithos 75, at a distance of 0.36 from its spout.
G.Kontomitsos/ classification 2, Christakopoulou – Somakou 2009, 300.	T104 (1999)	Tripod kettle/pot around of which six pouring and drinking vessels and a pyxis were found. Probably related to the dead of Tomb 85. It is not clear whether they were offerings for the dead or whether they constituted a distinct burial. The deposition of the pyxis as a non-bearing vase in pouring and drinking vessels enhances the use of the cookware as a burial pot.

Table 3. PYRES. Delineation. Correlation.

Property	Pyres	Delineation / Correlation
Chr. Kontomitsos / classification 2, Christakopoulou – Somakou 2009, 355.	Pyre 1 (1999)	1.42X1.33. Related to burials as it is 0.40 from T8 and 0.53 from T7. T-shaped. Covered with stone piles. Flanked by large stones. Pile of bones.
Chr. Kontomitsos / classification 2, Christakopoulou – Somakou 2009, 356.	Pyre 2 (1999)	1.42X0.67. Probably associated with the T17. Covered with stone pile on which burnt sherds were found.
Chr. Kontomitsos / classification 1, Christakopoulou – Somakou 2009, 371.	Pyre 3 (1999)	1.17X0.76. Found close to Pyre 2. Irregular shape and covered with stones. Above the stones, burnt soil, sherds and a Ψ type figurine.
Sp. Floros/ classification 2, Christakopoulou – Somakou 2009, 640.	Pyre 10/T318–T321	0.95X0.50. Irregular quadrilateral shape. Large rubble, burnt soil and sherds, a pin, a bronze ring and ceramic fragments were included. Related with the cremated dead contained within the vessel T318. The vessel 318 with the cremated dead, an oinochoe and a kantharos were incorporated into Pyre 10 that was held for him. Both Pyre 10 and T318 are related to burial 321.
Sp. Floros/ classification 2, Christakopoulou – Somakou 2009, 644.	Pyre 11/T321/TA	0.73X0.59. Irregular shape. Associated with the burial of T321/TA. Burnt bones and sherds.
Peslis/ classification 2, Christakopoulou – Somakou 2009, 711, 714.	Pyre 12/T378 (2000)	1.35X0.25X0.30–0.54. Quadrilateral shape. Charred material. Animal bones. Coal. The pyre is probably related to the bronze cauldron T378 found 0.50 deeper.
Peslis/ classification 2, Christakopoulou – Somakou 2009, 712.	Pyre/T376 (2000)	0.72X0.55. Quadrilateral shape. Three burned vessels based upright and incomplete from the height of the belly. Burned earth, crumbled burned bones. Two iron pins were found at the bottom of the larger vessel. One bronze ring was collected from the mound.
A.Koukouna/ classification 4, Christakopoulou – Somakou 2009, 986.	Pyre 7/T152 (1999)	Rectangular pit with single and double layer lining. Covered with a stone pile and a limestone slab. Within the pit burnt clay, charcoal and burnt bones, a bronze unidentified object, an iron spearhead and a bronze tweezers strain. All surfaces and objects were burnt. Related to Tomb 152, that was found right below.
A.Koukouna/ classification 4, Christakopoulou – Somakou 2009, 984.	Pyre 8/T133 (1999)	Rectangular pit lined with stones. Burnt clay and charcoal, burnt bone and shells, two copper rings corrupted by fire and irregular masses of iron incandescent, all covered with stone pile. It is related to the dead of pithos T133.

Table 3. PYRES. Delineation. Correlation.

Figure 22. Pyre 7 (of the 1998 excavation period). The handmade urn T54 that contained the ashes of the dead, probably was included in the remnants of the funeral feast.

In this category we must refer to Pyres 10 and 11 of the 1999 excavation period, related to the burial of the dead 318/321 and 321/TA respectively. These pyres were included in an individual cluster of relatives characterized by the use of different types of burial. More specifically Pyre 10 was associated with the cinerary urn 318, the burial pithos 321, the burial vessel (hydria) 321/TA, the stone built grave with the tripod pithos T322, and the burial pithos 319 (Figure 26-27). Of the former, only the dead of the tripod pithos 322 was found to be accompanied with weapons (Figure 27), confirming as such his position, and adding a further argument as to why this type of tomb was especially selected.

Pyre 10 (Figure 26) had an irregular quadrilateral shape and included large rubble, burnt clay and sherds as well as a pin, a bronze ring and ceramic fragments. The cremation of the dead T318 (found within Pyre 10) took place at an unspecified site, and then the ash vessel was incorporated into his/her burnt offerings. At the burial vessel 318 itself, the charred bones of the dead were accompanied by the characteristic pouring and drinking vessels, such as an oinochoe and a kantharos, while a clay lid, which initially sealed the urn, was found nearby. Completing the whole picture, a small limestone plaque found in the particular area, was placed as a burial signal. Right below Pyre 10 and the

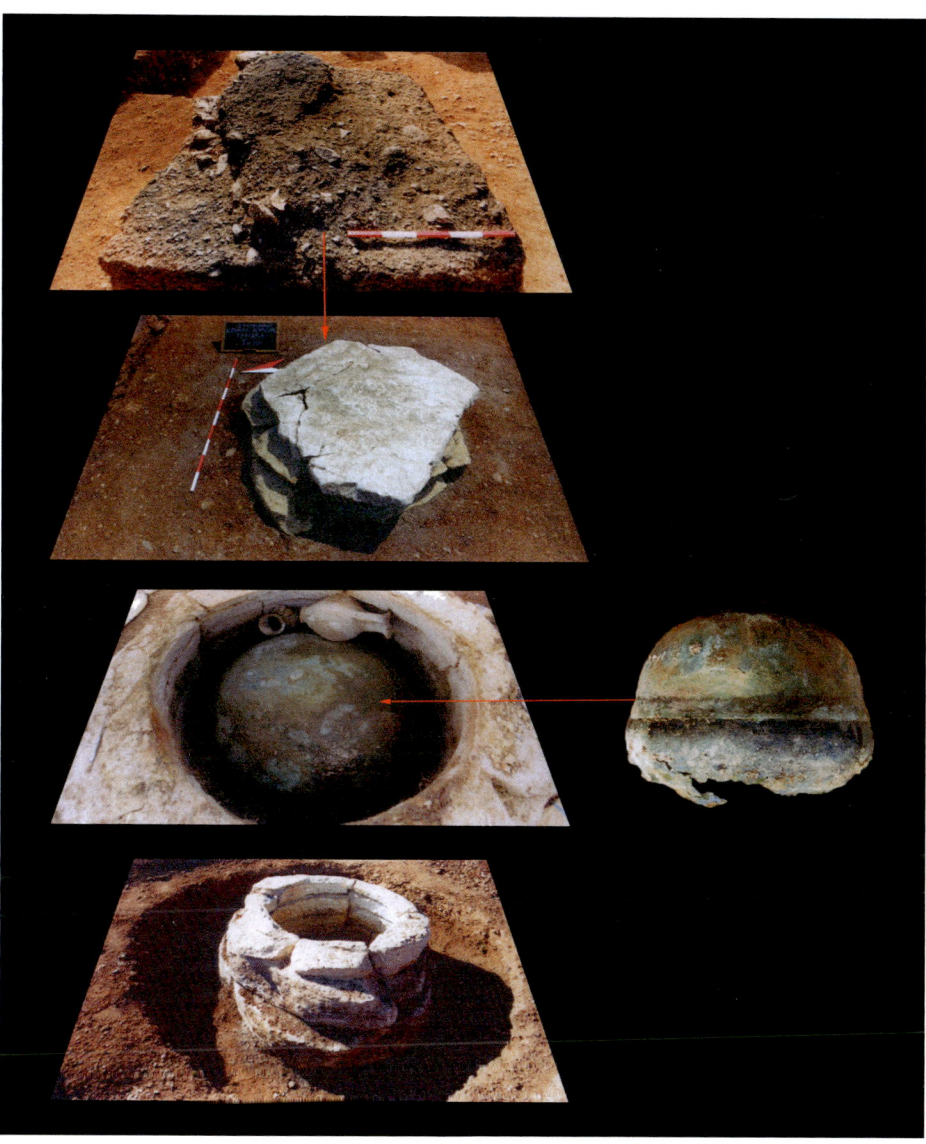

Figure 23. Pyre 12 and gradual discovery of the tomb T378 which the pyre covered.

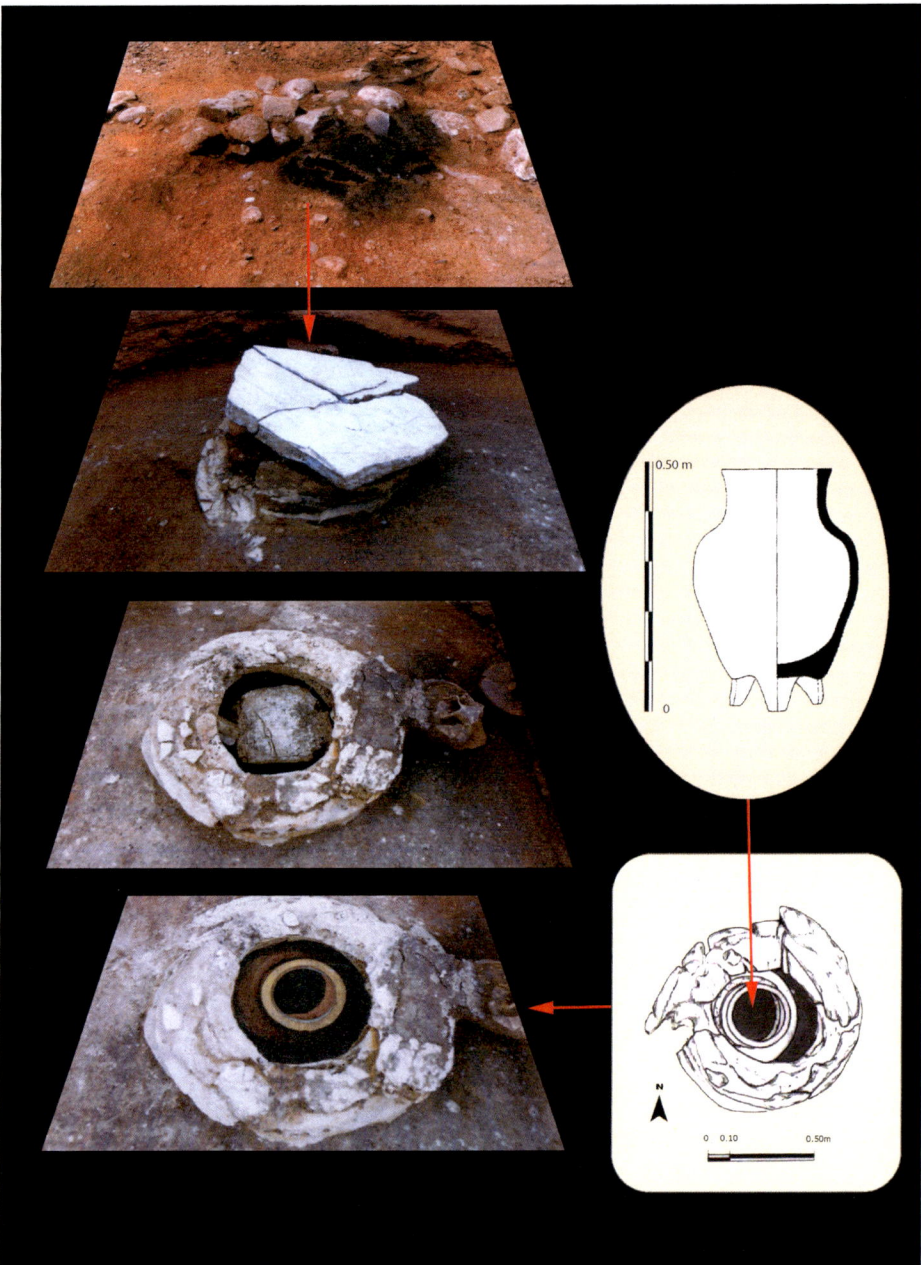

Figure 24. Pyre A and gradual discovery of the tomb T66 which the pyre covered.

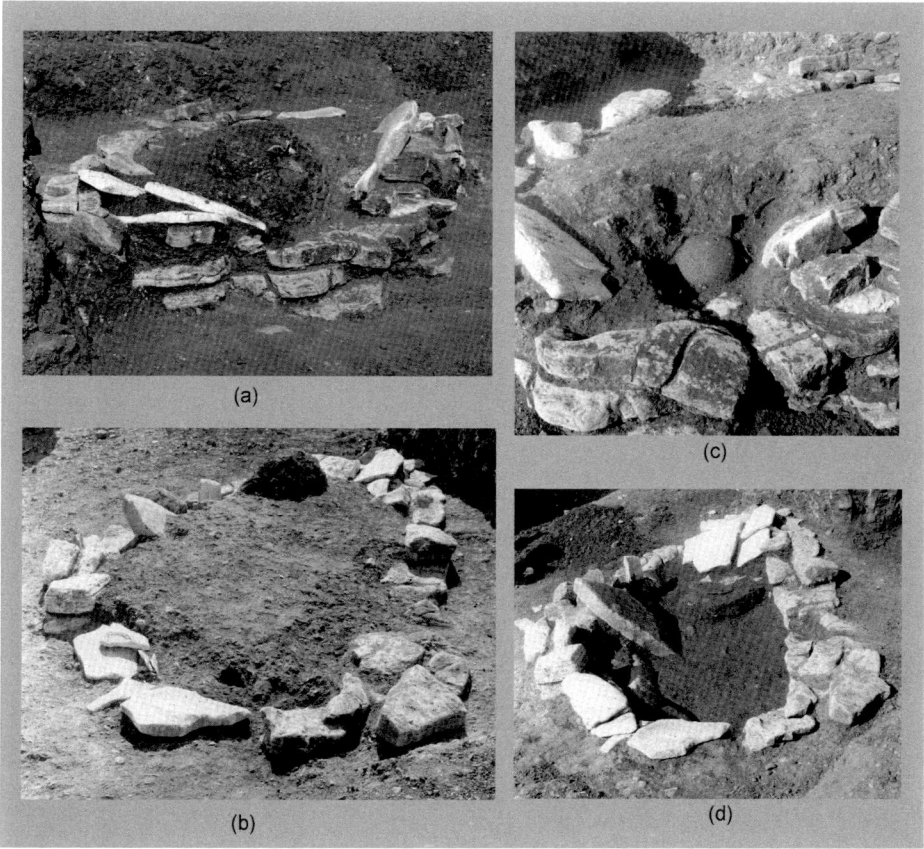

Figure 25. Apsidal tomb. Detail of the excavation where an ash layer and the fragments of two oinochoae (a), (c) are visible, relating to the burning debris of the clay tripod pithos (d). (b). The mound with the oinochoae from W.

burial vessel 318, a burial pithos T321 was revealed, directly associated with the aforementioned pyres.

Pyre 11 (Figure 27) was held for the burial of the dead T321/TA, which in turn accompanied the burial pithos 321.

The pyres A, B and C *(third category),* were found in Kostadima's property and as mentioned above belonged to the same cluster with the Kousarida's one. These were outlined by an angular structure which was arranged by sandstones, and in a direct but unambiguous relationship with the semicircular structures mentioned earlier (Figure 20). Perhaps the sandstones, constituted a burial enclosure that encircled the semicircular structures, graves and pyres as an

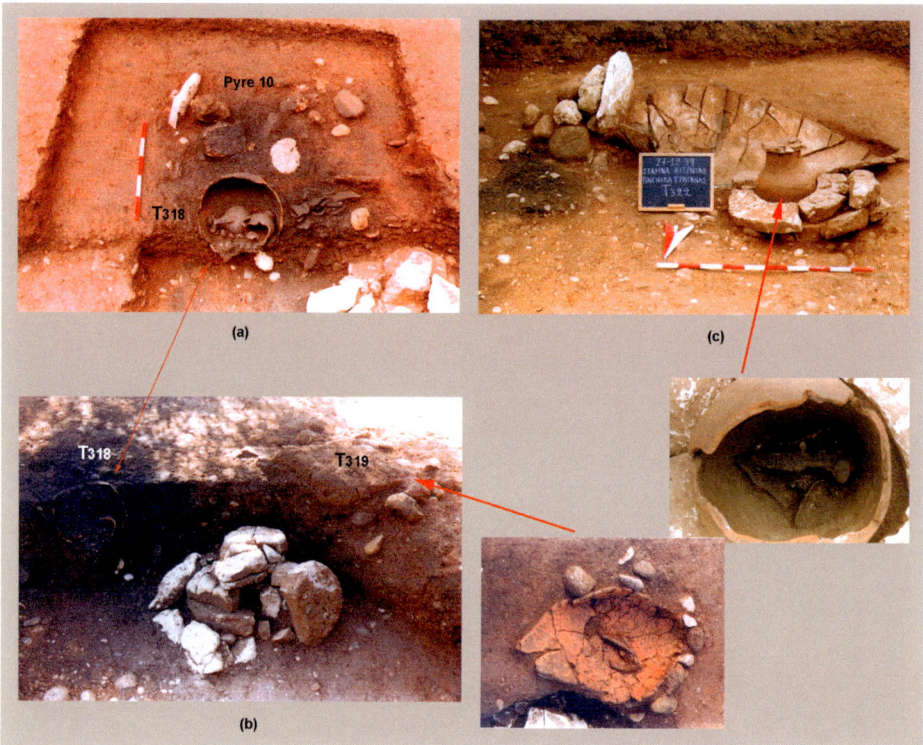

Figure 26. Pyre 10 (a) associated with the cinerary urn 318, the burial pithos 321 (c), the burial vessel (hydria) 321/TA (Figure 27), the stone built grave with the tripod pithos T322 (c), and the burial pithos 319 (b).

ensemble, which we can only speculate based on the data acquired so far. The presence of the Pyres in this area is probably connected with a ritual that concerns the whole cluster, with emphasis on collectivity, either in the form of the family or in the form of 'extended' families.

In the case of Pyres 7 (Figure 28) and 8 (Figure 29) recovered during the 1999-2000 excavation period, *(fourth category)* the typology, size and content of the pits was similar to pyres of individuals safely related with the owners of the tombs 152 and 133 respectively. If they were actually burial remains of cremations, to the identification of which directly contributed the deformed and fractured findings, the incinerated soil, the large amount of coal, all forming the result of a strong and long-lasting fire, then we face another peculiarity previously reported, as in Stamna the cremations took place outside the demarcated burial

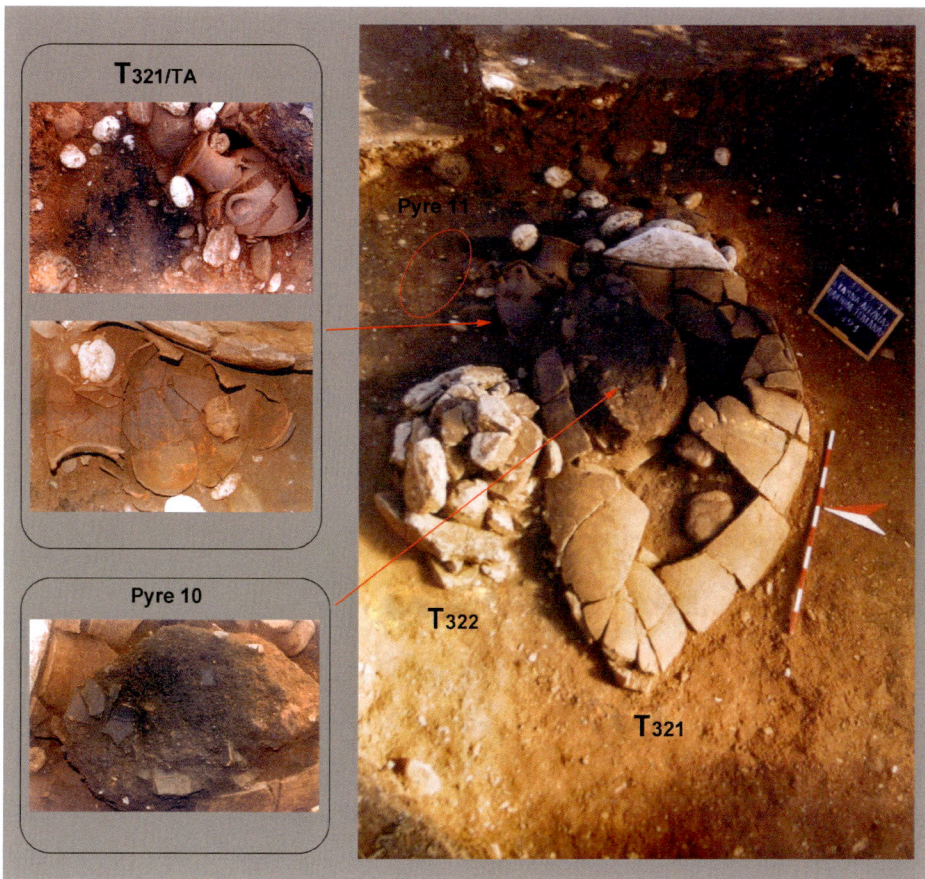

Figure 27. Pyres 10 and 11. Details. In the red circle the exact location of the Pyre 11 is noted. It is associated with the dead of hydria T321/TA.

clusters in places that have not been yet identified. Special reference should be made not only to Pyre's 7 position, immediately above the cist grave 152, but also to the position the iron leaf-shaped spear T7/2 (length 0.37m.) found, which intentionally demonstrated the tomb's position. Although is no gender identification of the dead available, from the immediacy of the pyre, the grave and the respective findings, one could argue that they were burials of people with close related bonds, for who cremation and inhumation were chosen respectively.

With regard to Pyre 8, the content of the pit where the intense heat has completely eroded the clay vessels and the copper rings found in the rusted soil, but also the ridge that has been carved around the pit, all witness the bygone existence of the probably wooden coverage, which in turn was covered by a

Figure 28. Pyre 7 (of the 1999-2000 excavation period). The recovery stages starting from the stone pile with which it was sealed and the presentation of the tomb 152, which the pyre itself accompanied.

Figure 29. Pyre 8 (of the 1999-2000 excavation period) and gradual discovery of the tomb T133.

large stone pile. Limestone slabs of small dimensions, of irregular and circular shape found between the respective stone pile of Pyres 7 and 8, intensified the 'sealing' of the pits, following perhaps a more traditional grave coverage pattern, as evidenced to date in Stamna.

The deposit of personal items such as jewelry (rings),[121] domestic tools (tweezers)[122] but also armor (spearhead)[123] by close relatives, within the cremation residues, differentiates their treatment by the depositors, as it is obvious that they were not only included in the main offerings of the tombs. Their inclusion in pyres and the intentional ending of their functional life, testify purification offerings for the exhilaration of both the deceased and their *providers*.

Summarizing, we could assume that the Stamna pyres could be considered, due to their limited number, to be a specialized offer that includes a lot of elements such as fire, funeral banquets, placing grave goods and vessel destruction during a ritual feasting,[124] which confirm a sequence of ceremonies with symbolic significance, including the (semi) circular stone constructions and the successive burial layers.

'Consuming' with the dead

In Stamna, the banquet ritual for the farewell of the deceased, as evidenced by the typology of the vessels contained in the graves, included mainly liquid consumption, and consisted, in their clear majority, of vessels for pouring and drinking. The excellent state of the vessels, in which there is no evidence of wearing or other evidence of daily use, directs us towards the existence of thriving local ceramic workshops with particularly stylistic features, as the hundreds of finds, of the also hundreds of tombs discovered and investigated, is not possible to have survived the movement of the population being included in the tombs after. It is obvious that many of the vessels were used exclusively for burial use, without necessarily having this prospect from the beginning.

The study of the material, as above cited, is an opportunity for asking the following questions:

---

[121] Christakopoulou 2009, 278.
[122] Christakopoulou 2009, 986-987.
[123] Christakopoulou 2009, 986-987.
[124] The finding sherds that do not make up for complete vessels in total, is evidence of the deposition of already fractured vessels, a ritual known from earlier periods.

1. Does the large number and the multiplicity of vases declare social differentiation but also racial representation of the members who took part in the ceremonial burial?[125] The typology of vessels which refers to Cypriot standards is one of the elements that are consistent with this.

2. Does the deceased receive multiple and different types of vessels from equally different holders who place a vase in his pile as the ultimate greeting? And does the deposit of limited number of vessels suggests a deliberate (in the form of an established ceremonial character) small gathering of participants in the ceremony;[126]

3. In the same logic and vice versa, a *large* accumulation of vases suggests a large gathering of participants, which displays automatically also the sociopolitical power of a specific group within the tribe, since participation in the funeral ritual was deemed necessary to strengthen its role? Yet on the other hand,

4. Does the *small* accumulation of vessels inside tombs with elaborate burial architecture implies exclusive and selective participation, as no one must prove to anyone that the dead belongs to the elite of the settlement?

The interpretation of the evidence is not an overall assessment in the form of integrated responses for all matters relating to this study, but it is sufficient for a first evaluation of the subject. More specifically, the large percentage of banquet vessels in the tombs of Stamna certainly implies the typical ceremonial farewell of the deceased from his relatives, and reflects a wider social context where the local elite was integrated and fully accepted by the population, so as to justify the post-mortem equation of ordinary citizens (at the standard ritual level), with it (the elite),[127] regardless of age. Wekowski, referring to Late Geometric Child Burial 168 in Pithekouses, which includes a significant number of drinking pots that do not respond to the young age of the deceased, justifies the submission of their offerings, approaching sociologically his cherished relatives. Specifically,*' to mark him off as a member of the social group that cherished the sympotic life style is clearly indicative of the ambitions of his family. In this particular*

---

[125] As mentioned in Christakopoulou 2016, 67, the Stamna society might have been heterogeneous, a fact which would be mainly reflected in burial customs and burial architecture.

[126] Kaskantiri 2017, 262-263, based on archaeological evidence of Mycenaean Krini, Achaia, argues that the small number of vessels accompanying the dead witnesses the low standard of living of most of the population, while in the contrary in Stamna it is more likely to be the result of a new ideological background that characterizes the Early Iron Age society.

[127] As Węcowski 2012, 24, points out with reference to Tomb 168 in Pithekousses, '*the families of a number of the dead in this necropolis seem to have wanted to emphasize that they belonged, or just aspired, to the group for whom ritual wine drinking was an important element of self-definition*'.

case, the relatives of the dead decided to symbolically outmatch all of their local peers.[128] In other words, by depositing these attributes that indicated participation in a banquet process, the relatives wanted to attribute symbolic values to a young person that otherwise would be given to a mature man (or woman?), values that were proved to belong to the elite of locals which rightfully had the right to this symbolism.

Moreover, the symbolic convivial character to which Węcowski refers[129] and is related to the deposit of a specific pair of vases, is also evident in Stamna with the exclusive deposition of a pair of vessels, consisting of a jug and an amphora, as in the case of the bronze cauldron T378 (Figure 10).

Burying the dead under the protective outer covering of bronze cauldrons and tripod jars that declare by themselves large scale feasting of their owners, while they were alive, does not necessary indicate a corresponding process (feasting) as part of the burial process, as evidenced by the scarce number of vessels within and outside the graves. *Pro rata* to earlier eras both in Crete and the mainland, Borgna reported that the Minoans approached the whole banquet ceremonial ritual differently than the Mycenaeans, by modifying and making it more extroverted, aiming at the substantial control of the society during the Post Palatial period, at a time of social and political instability.[130] As the banquet process in LHIIIC Asine took place behind closed doors and apparently with selected participants, in the Protogeometric period the process was much more open without excluding the possibility of religious rituals being carried out among the elites within the apsidal building, while at the same time the rest of the population was gathered outside.[131] Compared to the Mycenaean and the Minoan environment, the evidence for the elite's burials in Protogeometric Stamna so far, testify gatherings under the formal ritual of a banquet with clearly restrictive terms of major human involvement. By itself, the regular exclusion from everyday conventions, even from simple daily functions operates in terms of public psychology as a deterrent to the need for participation. The exclusion creates for ordinary citizens inferior feelings, which involve lack of confidence as a result of a negative psychology, operating positively in favor of the powerful.

---

[128] Węcowski 2012, 23-24.
[129] Węcowski 2012, 24, regarding the graves of San Montano mentions that although a large number of vessels were not deposited, however, the symbolic character of the banquet is evident, as can be seen from the placement of a jug and a cup as a typical pair: *'Therefore, I think we are entitled to conclude that less wealthy families did their best to meet aristocratic standards by imitating the symbols of the lifestyle of their more successful fellow-citizens'*.
[130] Borgna 2004, 256. For relevant bibliography see n.24. For substantial differences between the two cultures see Borgna 2004, 266 where the respective literature is cited.
[131] Livieratou 2011, 151.

Moreover, the force resulting from the strict setting of limits and decisions by small groups (whose members have the right to participate), defines its own social habits and behaviors. The purpose of these rituals is also to strengthen social behaviors that enhance the power of the elite, and keep in safe distance the population of a community in order to have sole control.[132]

Probably the whole process portrays the effect of an ideology clearly influenced by their migratory journey when instability and fear for the unknown restricted and simplified the formal ritual. The active involvement of the Stamna officials at such events and the tangible demonstration of their participation through the burial testimony, constitute elements of a *modus operandi* of a population with existing social structures and cultural norms, which obviously formed part of their tradition. In other words, the organization of the Stamna cemeteries, the architecture and the placement even of the most common of the graves, such as pithos tombs and shaft graves, reflect the strict structure of a hierarchically articulated society. Therefore, the securing of the latter, via the strengthening of a pre-existing, yet with a new operating mode, status, which is a result of the population movement, creates a dynamic stability factor.

As it has already been mentioned,[133] the cremation of the elites in combination with the placement of their ashes in tripod pithos/cauldrons (which testify their indefinite participation in banquets/feasts), which in turn are enclosed into peculiar architectural structures, confirms their superior position in the Early Iron Age hierarchy, as evidenced also in other regions. Along with the use of peculiar architectural constructions and the preference of cremation against the inhumation rite, we must consider the rate of human involvement and also the type and the percentage of the deposition of certain types of vessels, in order for their combination to direct us to reliable conclusions. According to this aspect, the inhabitants of Stamna, as in Pithikouses, had adopted and paid tribute to their beloved ones as if they had the right to participate in higher rating banquets. In reality though, and in actual banquets, they were not entitled to participate in this procedure because it was confined exclusively to the elite population.

Old cities, old souls…

The up to date published excavations, including remote settlements as shown in detail on the map (Figure 5) present a single geographic landscape where burial areas are demarcated under the model of a delineated residential settlement,

---

[132] As it becomes apparent from Fox's 2012, 36-40 excellent analysis that refers to the *'contsructed'* relationships between the *host* and the *guest*.
[133] Christakopoulou 2016, 60-61.

based, apparently, on a prototype spatial operating model. On this basis, Stamna is a key model for the regeneration of a settlement from which the inhabitants were initially moved in order to colonize this area.

A study on finding this model based on the typology of peculiar burial structures that have been researched to date has already preceded, demonstrating common elements with other regions and delineating possible sea and mountain routes.[134] Despite the overall presentation of the literature concerning these burial structures, it is evident, erroneously or not, that there is a special preference relating to burial cauldrons from West Gate Eretria. Their overall presence combined with the burial ritual and the powerful historical profile of PRG/G era in the Euboean, *ipso facto* leads us to a parallel comparison with the settlement in Stamna.

To the question why we look for a population movement from another geographic environment, while we could accept the evolution of the settlement from earlier times, a brief but comprehensive answer is summarized in the fact that despite the strong Mycenaean establishment in the wider area of Stamna, there is no representative Early Protogeometric appearance in total, as the abundance of graves dates back to Late Protogeometric times. In other words, a whole period is absent during which the inhabitants of the area, taking advantage of the powerful features of the Mycenaean payments and combining them with local or external characteristics, such as those from the neighboring Peloponnesus, would create a local rhythm with flourishing features that would smoothly evolve from the Early, resulting in the Late Protogeometric period. There would be thus successive phases, where their evolutionary typological procedure would be apparent.

On the contrary, a remarkable total of the Late Protogeometric period with improved features is presented (from which a question arises whether there was a route of evolutionary presence elsewhere) which, as has already been said, is now recognizable as the Protogeometric Aetolian rhythm.

The overall picture of the settlement, as shown from the study to date of the necropolis, reveals a population characterized by a sociopolitical model relatively ready and acceptable from all residents, regardless of the distance between the scattered settlements, but also from the central itself ,[135] as has been proven so far. This model is already hierarchically articulated and followed

---

[134] Christakopoulou 2016.
[135] The one comprised of Kousarida's / Kostadima's plots.

by an artistic integrity which renders that population group distinguishable, as opposed to others.

It is obvious that the populations that moved and established at Stamna were not just regional groups that sought a new place to develop and evolve. Furthermore, their presence in total reflects a stable and rich for its time social environment, the wider setting of which is visible through the burial sequence. The cultural, economic, and military elements, which evolved through the years, seem to have been already well-established in this population. The abundance of tombs, signifies an arithmetic sequence that reveals a large in scale settlement that was carried out sequentially, either from the inland or sea, within a reasonable time and without invasive character, but instead with absolute respect to the nature of preexisting communities of the Mycenaean period at the neighboring hill of St. Elias. That becomes evident by the Stamna tholos tomb,[136] as the last residence of one of the prominent inhabitants of the Protogeometric facility.

In a recent talk[137] concerning the fabrics that covered the tripod bronze cauldron 587,[138] K. Sarri reports[139] that radiocarbon dating of the samples, places their manufacture before 1000BC,[140] a dating that according to the researcher is justified if a) they were offered to the deceased as family heirlooms,[141] since they were earlier than the burial[142] b) the burial itself is earlier and it is dated at the end of the Sub-Mycenaean and in the beginning of the Protogeometric era,[143] c) leads to a revision of the chronological limits for the period: *the chronological system of Aetolia as a whole is a subject to be revised in order to place Aetolia at the outset of protogeometric evolution along or approximately Argolida and Attica*.[144] Regardless of the dating of the offerings,[145] the following assumption

---

[136] For relevant literature about the tholos tomb see Christakopoulou 2016, 62, n.18.
[137] The speech was part of a Workshop/Meeting on Ancient Fabric that was held from the Athens National Archaeological Museum (2016/12/09) by Dr. K. Sarri, under the *title* 'Υφαίνουσιν αλιπόρφυρα': υφάσματα από το Πρωτογεωμετρικό Νεκροταφείο της Σταμνάς.
[138] See also Kolonas, L., Sarri, K., Skals, I., Margariti, Chr., Vanden Berghe, I. & Nosch, M.L. *Protogeometric Funerary Textiles from Stamna, Aitolia, Greece*. NESAT XII (Poster presentation).
[139] http://www.blod.gr/lectures/Pages/viewlecture.aspx?LectureID=3170
[140] http://www.blod.gr/lectures/Pages/viewlecture.aspx?LectureID=3170, 12.56-13.20min.
[141] http://www.blod.gr/lectures/Pages/viewlecture.aspx?LectureID=3170, 14.00-14.07 min. For depositing heirlooms in later graves see, Alexandridou 2016, 350 with relevant bibliography.
[142] In theory, and in accordance to the traditional dating system, http://www.blod.gr/lectures/Pages/viewlecture.aspx?LectureID=3170, 12.56-13.20min.
[143] http://www.blod.gr/lectures/Pages/viewlecture.aspx?LectureID=3170, 14.10-14.25 min.
[144] http://www.blod.gr/lectures/Pages/viewlecture.aspx?LectureID=3170, 14.26 - 14.45min...'ολόκληρο το συμβατικό χρονολογικό σύστημα στην Αιτωλία να επιδέχεται αναθεώρησης ώστε να τοποθετεί την Αιτωλία στην πρώτη γραμμή των πρωτογεωμετρικών εξελίξεων μαζί με την Αργολίδα και την Αττική ή κοντά σε αυτές'
[145] Unfortunately enough, the results of the dating of the finds are still pending, therefore no further data is available on the subject.

can be made: similarities concerning the burial customs and the typology of the tombs of the Stamna population, especially with those in Lefkandi and Eretria, spontaneously lead us to wonder if the people who came to the area probably from the north, and belonged to a joint team, at some point and for unknown reasons they diverged and, following alternative routes, arrived in Euboea and the wider area of Stamna, at a different time. As I argued in my previous article,[146] during a population movement, it is much more likely that the memories of burial customs would be preserved in the symbolic form of the typology of tombs and in the cult process, and not in perishable domestic objects which would be replaced and re-created following new types, influenced by the local pottery and which would now serve new necessities. Under this perspective and with reference to the pottery of Stamna the typological data, which are similar to the pottery of Lefkandi, is justified as an echo of a common origin and route, that as it diversified, it led to the creation of a new discrete ceramic typology. This rationale is also been reinforced by the dating of the fabrics, agreeing to K. Sarri's terms, according to which Aetolia is likely to be placed in the forefront of habitation in relation to the known populations of the Protogeometric period.

'In Darkness We Trust'

Symposium in life and death is a timeless tradition that as a post mortem ritual process has evolved in the Protogeometric era in Stamna, under conditions and with modifications required by the residents. Obviously, the logic of the process is identical to that found in other parts of Greece and abroad, but it shows variations due to the improvisation and the sensitivity of the persons concerned.

1. It is most likely for the wider population of Stamna to include drinking consumption as a formal burial custom, as evidenced by the apposition of drinking sets that have been found in tombs under study, while only the elite of the settlements, were legalized to host such gatherings, as can be seen from the limited and hence exclusive use of burial ceramic tripod (or no) pots and cauldrons, in order to emphasize their own personality over the whole cluster, of which they constituted active members. At the same time, however, they also aim to highlight and exaggerate the collective nature of the family to which they belong ensuring and protecting their authorities over other family clusters of Stamna.

---
[146] Christakopoulou 2016, 61-62.

2. Symposium in Stamna seems to be essentially the means with which the host demonstrates and validates his socio-political/military superiority over the participants, but also over those who attend but are not entitled to participate. The burial ceremony comprising with drinking and eating consumption, including domestic and other items that are used in banquets, is an institutional ritual in the form of the tangible continuity of the supremacy of the *once in life* banquet host, both in the world of the dead, but also in the world of the living, which is achieved (in the latter case) with the mightiness of a powerful memory.[147] The strengthening of the memory of the deceased Stamna's official activates in turn a process of enhancing the status and empowerment of his own family if his authority is hereditary.

3. As in the case of pottery which forms a tangible and readable part of the identity of a civilization, likewise in the institutional part that characterizes the sociopolitical identity of Stamna, the origin of features deriving from an earlier society is also readable. Indeed, in Stamna, the perception of a pre-existing and already established ideological notion concerning the burial practice mentioned above is diffused. The use of tripod cauldrons and tripod clay jars is not an imitation but an evolutionary continuity of a Sub-Mycenaean society whose elements are still either hidden or they do not exist anymore, but belong to populations displaced from elsewhere and settled in this area. Nevertheless, small or large-scale banqueting in life and death and the procedure followed in order to achieve it, is one of the processes that integrates Stamna's society into the profile of the Early Iron Age societies of other regions such as Lefkandi, Eretria, Attica and elsewhere. The placement itself of distinctive burial constructions of officials among the graves of ordinary people and not in separate and prominent locations is typical of the era, forming a result of the abolition of the central power of the Mycenaeans and of the realignment imposed.

4. Symposium and the parallel use of large tripod vessels with burial function, in conjunction with the use of pouring and drinking vessels intensify the recognition of the dead with the attribute of a senior official, as quoted in the various historical sources, giving supremacy in the region and its inhabitants.

5. The dating of the offerings that comprised of cauldrons and tripod jars is older than that of metal urns of the Iron Age in Greece, Cyprus and

---

[147] For the connection of the living and the dead through food consumption in mortuary contexts and its social meaning see Hamilakis 1998, with relevant bibliography.

Italy.¹⁴⁸ Clearly there are earlier cremations in metal urns in Spaliareika at Lousika in Achaia, or Cyprus and Crete or in Lefkandi,¹⁴⁹ but specifically the typology of the bronze cauldron integrated in a built structure finds relatively equivalent, of subsequent years mainly in Eretria where likewise a hemispherical cavity has been carved to integrate and stabilize burial cauldrons.

6. However, the finding in the area under study of a multitude of tombs reflects a clear strong and prosperous culture of the Iron Age, which operates strictly in relation to the norms of its time, as those have already formed based on the standards in Lefkandi and Eretria, and on a population scale that is far greater than that of the already known areas. The strengthening of the status of this powerful population demanded, among other, war readiness, as evidenced by the presence of war equipment in graves- but also a connotation of high-ranking military hierarchy that carried out large scale feasts.

7. The transfer of the rite of the banquet as a social event with political implications which goes back to the secular sphere, in the private circle, as it now involved a limited number of people, is considered an influence of the Mycenaean civilization.¹⁵⁰ This *metathesis* also entails the transfer of the wealth that characterizes the elite's gatherings, with all its socio-political implications at a grave level so that the status of the predominant of the population is recognized also after death, as is also the case for the warriors.¹⁵¹

Finding and studying such large number of tombs of the era, constitutes a remarkable representative example for discussing the administration of death, its confrontation through the ritual of mourning, and the creation of an individual and collective memory of the population that operated in the privileged geographic settlement of Stamna, redefining the cultural landscape of the Protogeometric era. The pre-existing theoretical framework (in the sense of timeless thinking), the methodology of managing and the display of grief and their correlation with already studied and exalted geographical parallels, integrate Stamna into the cultural chain of the populations ruled by an overall/systematic design of a particular cultural ideology. This cultural ideology seems to be interpreted and treated differently, which is justified by the delay that individual populations suffered, when moving from their original cradle and

---

[148] See Crielaard 2016, 49, table 1.
[149] Ibid.
[150] Borgna 2004, 268.
[151] Borgna 2004.

until their final settlement, the formation of their social composition and the standardization of their living conditions.

Figure 30. Pithos T55/1998.

Figure 31. Pithos T13/1998.

Figure 32. Cist grave T49/1999.

Figure 33. Pithos T38/1998.

Figure 34. Pithos T58/1999.

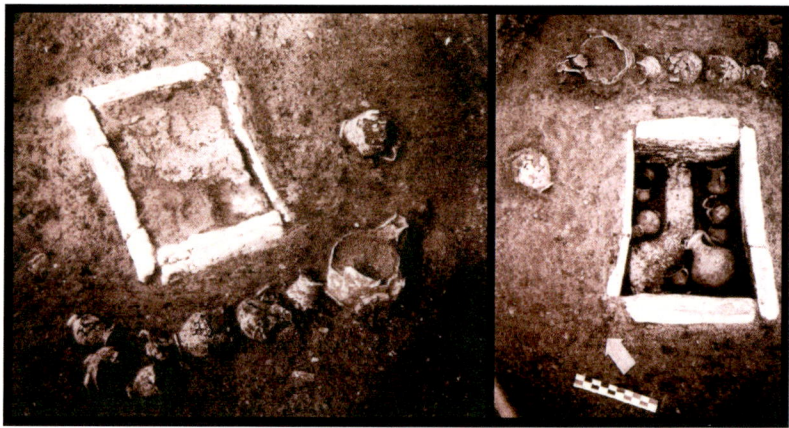

Figure 35. Cist grave T21/1998.

Figure 36. Cist grave T56/1998.

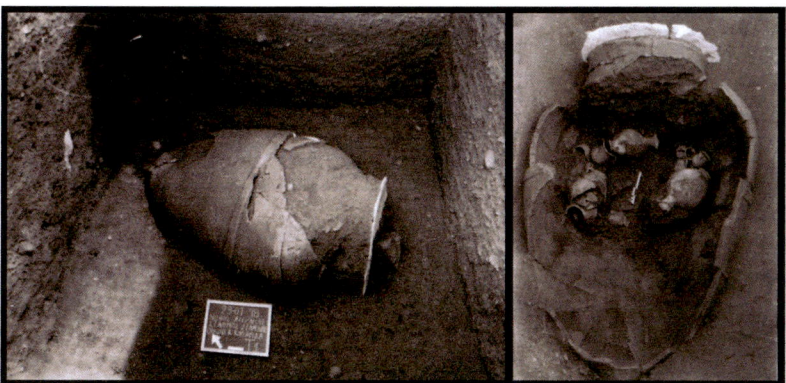

Figure 37. Pithos T1/1998.

Figure 38. Two handled pithos T11/1998.

Figure 39. Built shaft tomb 66.

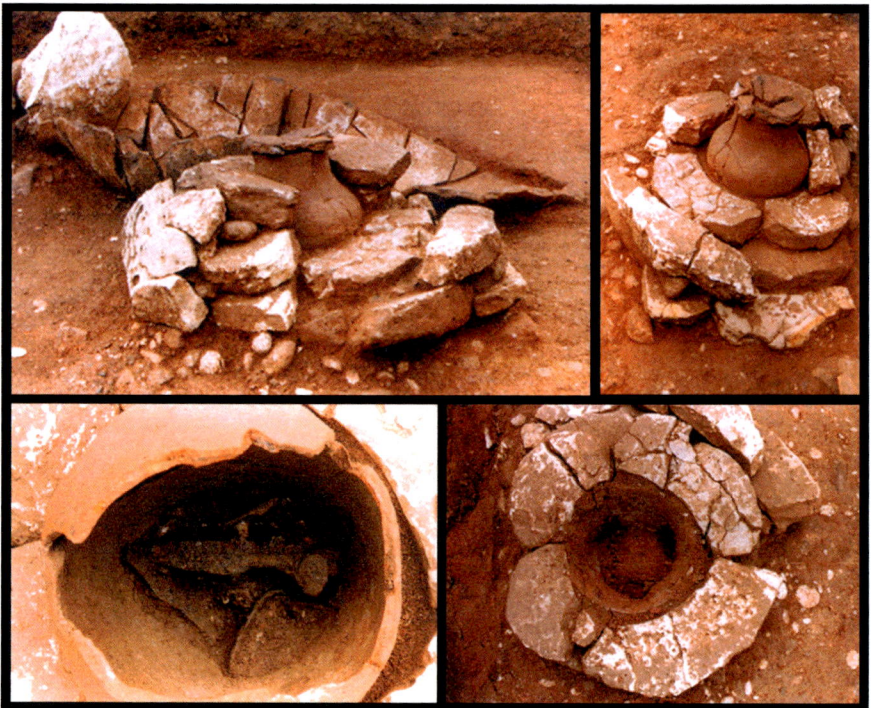

Figure 40. Built shaft tomb 322.

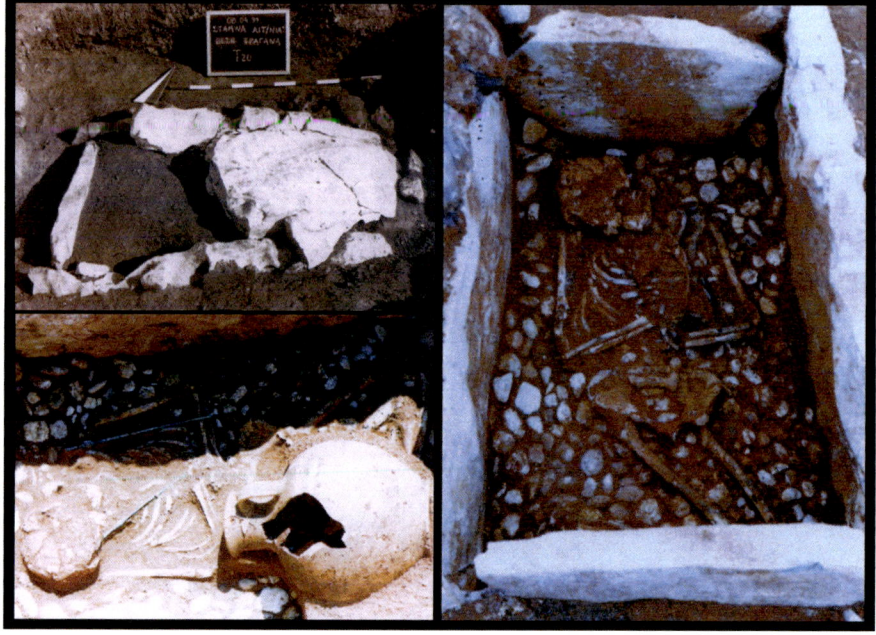

Figure 41. Cist grave T20/1999.

Figure 42. Pithos T63/1998.

Figure 43. Pithos T133/1999.

Figure 44. Cist grave T227.

Figure 45. Cist grave T35/1999.

Figure 46. Pithos T385.

References

Alexandridou, A. 2016. Funerary Variability in Late Eighth-Century B.C.E. Attica (Late Geometric II). *American Journal of Archaeology* 120, No. 3 (July 2016): 333–360.

Antonaccio, M.C. 1995. *An Archaeology of Ancestors. Tomb Cult and Hero Cult in Early Greece.* Lanham 1995.

Arnold, B. 2001. Power drinking in Iron Age Europe, in British Archaeology 57:11-19, available from: https://www.academia.edu/358441/Power_Drinking_In_Iron_Age_Europe

Barrowclough, D. 2014. Bronze Age Feasting Equipment: A contextual discussion of the Salle and East Anglian cauldrons and flesh-hooks, available from: https://www.academia.edu/8068486/Bronze_Age_Feasting_Equipment_A_contextual_discussion_of_the_Salle_and_East_Anglian_cauldrons_and_flesh-hooks

Borgna, E. 1997. Kitchen-Ware from LM IIIC Phaistos: Cooking Traditions and Ritual Activities in LBA Cretan Societies. *Studi Micenei ed Egeo Anatolici* 39: 189-217.

Borgna, E. 2003. *Il complessodi ceramica TM III dell' Acropoli Medianad i Festas (scavi 1955)* (Studi di archeologia cretese 3). Catania.

Borgna, E. 2004. Aegean feasting. A Minoan perspective. *Hesperia* 73: 247-279, available from: https://www.academia.edu/3560673/Aegean_Feasting_A_Minoan_Perspective

Brouwers, J.J. 2010. Warfare and Society in Early Greece. From the fall of the Mycenaean palaces to the end of the Persian wars. Academisch Proefchrift, Vrije Universiteit Amsterdam.

Carter, J. B. 1997. Thyasos and Marzeah: Ancestor Cult in the Age of Homer, in Langdon, S. (ed) *New Light on a Dark Age: Exploring the Culture of Geometric Greece*: 72-112. Columbia, Mo.

Cavanagh, W.G. and Mee, Chr. 1998. *A Private Place: Death in Prehistoric Greece* (Studies in Mediterranean Archaeology 125). Jonsered.

Charalambidou, X. 2008-2009. The Pottery from the Early Iron Age Necropolis of Tsikalario on Naxos: Preliminary Observations. *Annali dell'Istituto Universitario Orientale di Napoli* 15-16: 57-69, available from: https://www.academia.edu/3191233/X._Charalambidou_The_pottery_from_the_Early_Iron_Age_necropolis_of_Tsikalario_on_Naxos_preliminary_observations_AION_Annali_dell_Istituto_Universitario_Orientale_di_Napoli_no._15-16_2008-2009_pp._57-69

Charalambidou, X. 2011. Quantitative analysis of the pottery from the Early Iron Age necropolis of Tsikalario on Naxos, in Verdan, S., Theurillat, Th. and Kenzelmann Pfyffer, A. (eds) *Early Iron Age Pottery: A quantitative approach. Proceedings of the International Round Table organized by the Swiss School of archaeology in Greece* (Athens, November 28-30, 2008): 139-47. Oxford, available from: https://www.academia.edu/3191082/X._

Charalambidou_Quantitative_analysis_of_the_pottery_from_the_Early_Iron_Age_necropolis_of_Tsikalario_on_Naxos_in_S.Verdan_Th.Theurillat_A.Kenzelmann_Pfyffer_eds_Early_Iron_Age_Pottery_A_quantitative_approach..._Oxford_2011_pp._139-47

Charalambidou, X. 2012. Κεραμικά ευρήματα από τη νεκρόπολη του Τσικαλαριού στη Νάξο: Παρατηρήσεις σχετικά με το ταφικό περιβάλλον και τη χρήση των ευρημάτων. *Αρχαιογνωσία* 16, Vol. 1-3 2010-2012: 149-186. Athens, available from: http://www.academia.edu/3190900/X._Charalambidou_

Christakopoulou, G. 2001. Πρωτογεωμετρικός τάφος στη Σταμνά Μεσολογγίου, in Stampolidis, N. Chr. (ed.) *Cremations in Bronze and Early Iron Age, Proceedings of International Symposium* (Rhodes, 29/4-2/5 1999): 155-168. Athens, available from: https://www.academia.edu/2408644/2001.

Christakopoulou, G. 2006. Σωστικές ανασκαφές στη Σταμνά και το Αγγελόκαστρο Αιτωλοακαρνανίας. *Πρακτικά της Ά Αρχαιολογικής Συνόδου Νότιας και Δυτικής Ελλάδος, Πάτρα* 9-12 Ιουνίου 1996: 511-518. Athens, available from: https://www.academia.edu/2408701/2006.

Christakopoulou–Somakou, G. 2009. Το Νεκροταφείο της Σταμνάς και η Πρωτογεωμετρική περίοδος στην Αιτωλοακαρνανία. Unpublished PhD dissertation, National and Kapodistrian University of Athens, available from: http://thesis.ekt.gr/thesisBookReader/id/18271#page/1/mode/2up

Christakopoulou, G. 2016. The Protogeometric settlement at Stamna, Aetolia. Some thoughts on the settlers' origin based on the typology of the graves, in Papadopoulou Chrysikopoulou, E., Chrysikopoulos, V. and Christakopoulou, G. (eds) *ACHAIOS, Studies presented to Professor Thanasis I. Papadopoulos.* (Archaeopress Archaeology): 59-76. Oxford.

Coldstream, J.N. 2011. Geometric Elephantiasis, in Mazarakis Ainian, A. (ed.) *The 'Dark Ages' Revisited: An International Conference in Memory of William D.E. Coulson, Volos, 14-17 June 2007*: 801–5. Volos: University of Thessaly Press.

Corner, S. 2015. Symposium, in Wilkins, J. and Nadeau, R. (eds) *A Companion to Food in the Ancient World*: 234-242. UK.

Crielard, P. J. 2006. Basileis at Sea: Elites and External Contacts in the Euboian Gulf Region from the End of the Bronze Age to the Beginning of the Iron Age, in Deger Jalkotzy, S. and Lemos, S.I. (eds) *Ancient Greece: From The Mycenaean Palaces to the Age of Homer*: 271-297. Edinburgh: Edinburgh University Press.

Crielard, P. J. 2007. Eretria's West Cemetery revisited: burial plots, social structure and settlement organization during the 8th and 7th centuries BC, in Mazarakis Ainian, A. (ed) *Oropos and Eyboea in the Early Iron Age, Acts of an International Round Table, University of Thessaly June 18-20, 2004*: 169-194. Volos: University of Thessaly Press, available from: https://www.academia.edu/2379040/Eretria_s_West_Cemetery_revisited_burial_plots_social_structure_and_settlement_organization_during_the_8th_and_7th_centuries_BC_2007_

Crielard, P. J. 2013. Keleutha Hygra. Maritime Matters and the Ideology of Seafaring in the Greek Epic Tradition, in *Alle origini della Magna Greci, Mobilita Migrazioni Fondazioni, Atti del cinquantesimo convegno di studi sulla Magna Grecia, Aranto 1-4 Ottobre 2010*: 135-157. Istituto per la Storia e l'Archeologia della Magna Grecia – TarantoMMXII, available from: https://www.academia.edu/3541850/Keleutha_Hygra._Maritime_Matters_and_the_Ideology_of_Seafaring_in_the_Greek_Epic_Tradition_2013_

Crielard, P.J. 2016. Living heroes: Metal urn cremations in Early Iron Age Greece, Cyprus and Italy, in Gallo, F. (ed) *Omero: quaestiones disputata* (Ambrosiana Graecolatina 5): 43-78. Milano & Roma, Biblioteca Ambrosiana - Bulzoni Editore, available from: https://www.academia.edu/30379083/Living_heroes_metal_urn_cremations_in_Early_Iron_Age_Greece_Cyprus_and_Italy_2016_

Dabney, M.K. and Wright, C.J. 1990. Mortuary Customs, Palatial Society and State Formation in the Aegean Area: A Comparative Study, in Hägg, R., and Nordquist, C. G. (eds) *Celebrations of Death and Divinity in the Bronze Age Argolid.* (Proceedings of the Sixth International Symposium at the Swedish Institute at Athens 40): 45-53. Stockholm.

Dabney, K.M., Halstead, P. and Thomas, P. 2004. Mycenaean feasting on Tsoungiza at Ancient Nemea. *Hesperia* 73: 197-215.

Dakoronia, F. 2006. Early Iron Age Elite Burials in East Lokris, in Deger Jalkotzy, S. and Lemos, S.I. (eds) *Ancient Greece: From the Mycenaean Palaces to the Age of Homer*: 483–504 . Edinburgh.

Dakouri-Hild, A. 2016. Getting to Funerary Place in a Fairly Short Stretch of Time: Death and Performance in the Prehistoric Aegean, in Dakouri-Hild, A. and Boyd, Michael, J. (eds) *Staging Death. Funerary Performance, Architecture and Landscape in the Aegean.* Berlin/Boston.

de Fidio, P. 2001. Centralization and its Limits in the Mycenaean Palatial System, in Voutsaki, S. and Killen, J. (eds) *Economy and Politics in the Mycenaean Palace States* (Cambridge Philological Society, Suppl.27): 15-24. Cambridge.

Dickinson, O.T.P.K. 2006. *The Aegean from Bronze Age to Iron Age: Continuity and Change Between the Twelfth and Eighth Centuries BC.* London.

Eder, B. and Jung, R. 2005. On the Character of Social Relations between Greece and Italy in the 12th/11th centuries BC, in Laffineur, R. and Greco, E. (eds) *Emporia, Aegeans in the Central and Eastern Mediterranean* (Proceedings of the 10th International Aegean Conference/10ᵉ Rencontre Égéenne Internationale Athens, Italian School of Archaeology, 14-18 April 2004): 485-495.

Enverova, Deniz, A. 2012. From Bronze Age to Iron Age in the Aegean: A Heterarchical Approach, Department of Archaeology İhsan Doğramacı Bilkent University Ankara.

Erickson, E.B. 2010. Priniatikos Pyrgos and the Classical period in Eastern Crete. Feasting and Island Identities, *Hesperia* 79: 305-349, available from http://www.ascsa.edu.gr/pdf/uploads/hesperia/40981053.pdf

Fox, S.R. 2012. *Feasting Practices and Changes in Greek Society from the Late Bronze Age to Early Iron Age* (BAR International Series 2345). Oxford.

Gadolou. A. 2017. Δύο κρατήρες Πρώιμων Ιστορικών Χρόνων από την Αχαΐα. Εκφράσεις κοινωνικής διαφοροποίησης και εδραίωσης της συλλογικής ταυτότητας στη διάρκεια του 8ου αι. π.Χ, in Vlachou, V. and Gadolou, A. (eds) *ΤΕΡΨΙΣ, Studies in Mediterranean Archaeology in honour of Nota Kourou* (Etudes d' Archeologie 10): 47-60. Brussels.

Gerloff, S. 1986. Bronze Age Class A Cauldrons: Typology, Origins and Chronology. *Journal of the Royal Society of Antiquaries of Ireland* 116:84-115.

Gerloff, S. 2010. *Atlantic Cauldrons and Buckets of the Late Bronze Age and Early Iron Ages in Western Europe* (Prähistorische Bronzefunde II, 18). Stuttgart.

Hägg, R. 1990. The role of libations in Mycenaean ceremony and cult, in Celebrations of death and divinity in the Bronze Age Argolid. Proceedings of the Sixth International Symposium at the Swedish Institute at Athens, 11–13 June, 1988 (ActaAth-4°, 40):177–184. Stockholm.

Hägg, I. 1994. Kultgebräuche im Alpenraum und in der Ägäis. Zur Frage der Funktion der Feuerböcke aus Eschenz, in Schmid.-Sikimić, B. and Della Casa, P. (eds) *Trans Europam. Beiträge zur Bronze und Eisenzeit zwischen Atlantik und Altai. Festschrift für Margarita Primas* (Antiquitas, Reihe 3, Band 34): 211–234. Bonn.

Halstead., P. 2012. Feast, Food and Fodder in Neolithic-Bronze Age Greece. Commensality and the Construction of Value. *eTopoi. Journal for ancient Studies* II: 21-51, available from: http://journal.topoi.org/index.php/etopoi/article/view/34/93

Hamilakis, Y. 1998. Eating the dead: mortuary feasting and the politics of memory in the Aegean Bronze Age, in Branigan, K. (ed) *Cemetery and Society in the Aegean Bronze Age Societies*: 115-132. Sheffield: Sheffield Academic Press. available from: https://www.academia.edu/250471/Hamilakis_Y._1998._Eating_the_dead_mortuary_feasting_and_the_politics_of_memory_in_the_Aegean_Bronze_Age._In_Branigan_K._ed_Cemetery_and_Society_in_the_Aegean_Bronze_Age_societies._Sheffield_Sheffield_Academic_Press

Hamilakis, Y. and Sherratt, S. 2012. Feasting and the consuming body in Bronze Age Crete and Early Iron Age Cyprus, in Cadogan, G., Kopaka, K., Iacovou, M. and Whitley, J. (eds) *Parallel Lives: Ancient Island Societies in Crete and Cyprus 3000-300 BC*: 187-207, available from: http://www.academia.edu/2224501/Feasting_and_the_consuming_body_in_Bronze_Age_Crete_and_Early_Iron_Age_Cyprus_by_Y._Hamilakis_and_S._Sherratt

Iakovides, S. 1980. *Excavations of the Necropolis at Perati*. Los Angeles.

Isaakidou, V., Halstead, P., Davis, J. and Stocker, S. 2002. Burnt animal sacrifice at the Mycenaean Palace of Nestor, Pylos. *Antiquity* 76: 86-92.

Kaskantiri, S. 2017. Τα μυκηναϊκά νεκροταφεία στις θέσεις Ζωητάδα και Άγιος Κωνσταντίνος στην Κρήνη Πατρών. Unpublished PhD dissertation, available from: http://thesis.ekt.gr/thesisBookReader/id/40585#page/1/mode/2up

Knapp, A.B. 1986. *Copper Production and Divine Protection: Archaeology, Ideology and Social Complexity on Bronze Age Cyprus* (Studies in Mediterranean Archaeology Pocket-Book 42). Göteborg.

Knapp, A.B. 2006. Orientalization and Prehistoric Cyprus: The Social Life of Oriental Goods, in Riva, C. and Vella, C.N. (eds) *Debating Orientalization: Multidisciplinary Approaches to Processes of Change in the Ancient Mediterranean* (Monographs in Mediterranean Archaeology): 48–65. London.

Kontorli-Papadopoulou, L. 2017. Ανασκάπτοντας στην Ομηρική Ιθάκη. Αποτελέσματα ανασκαφικού - ερευνητικού προγράμματος του Πανεπιστημίου

Ιωαννίνων στη Βόρεια Ιθάκη, in *Δωδώνη, Ιστορία και Αρχαιολογία , Τεύχος Α, ΤΟΜΟΣ ΜΓ΄ - ΜΔ΄* (2014-2015): 467-504. Ioannina.
Kourou, N. 1999. *Ανασκαφές Νάξου. Το Νότιο Νεκροταφείο της Νάξου κατά τη Γεωμετρική περίοδο*. Athens.
La Rosa, V., Palermo, D. and Vagnetti, L. (eds) 1999. *Επί πόντον πλαζόμενοι: Simposio italiano di studi egei dedicato a Luigi Bernabó Brea e Giovanni Pugliese Carratelli*. Roma.
Levi, D. 1961-1962. La tomba a tholos di Kamilari presso Festos. *Annuario della Scuola archeologica di Atene e delle Missioni italiane in Oriente* 39-40:7-148.
Levi, D. 1976. *Festas e la civilta minoica 1*. Rome.
Livieratou, A. 2011. Regional cult systems in the transitional period from the Late Bronze to the Early Iron Age: Comparing the evidence from two different parts of Mainland Greece, the Argolic plain and East Phokis, in Mazarakis Ainian, A. (ed) *The Dark Ages Revisited, Acts of an international Symposium in memory of William D.E Coulson* (University of Thessaly Volos, 14-17 June, VII): 147-164. Volos.
Lloyd, M. 2015. Death of a Swordsman, Death of a Sword: The Killing of Swords in the Early Iron Age Aegean (ca. 1050 to ca.690 B.C.E), in Geoff, L., Whittaker, H. and Wrightson, G. (eds) *Ancient Warfare: Introducing Current Research* Volume I. Cambridge.
Luce, J.M. 2011. From miniature objects to giant ones: The process of defunctionalisation in sanctuaries and graves in Iron Age Greece, The Gods of Small Things. *Pallas* 86: 53-73, available from: https://journals.openedition.org/pallas/2096
O' Connor, Kaori. 2015. *The Never-ending Feast: The Anthropology and Archaeology of Feasting*. London–New York.
Mazarakis Ainian, A. 2009. Αρχιτεκτονική και Ιστορία κατά τους Πρώιμους Ιστορικούς Χρόνους. *Αρχαιολογία και Τέχνες* 112.18-30.
Maran, J. and Stavrianopoulou, E. 2007. Πότνιος Ανήρ. Reflection of the Ideology of the Mycenaean Kingship, in Alram-Stern, E. and Nightingale, G. (eds) *Keimelion: Elitenbildung und elitärer Konsum von der mykenischen Palastzeit bis zur homerischen Epoche* (Akten des internationalen Kongresses vom 3. bis 5. Februar 2005 in Salzburg, Wien): 285-298. Wien.
Maran, J. 2012. Ceremonial Feasting Equipment, Social Space and Interculturality in Post-Palatial Tiryns, in Maran, J. and Stockhammer, W.Ph. (eds) *Materiality and Social Practice, Transformative Capacities of Intercultural Encounters*: 121-136. Oxford and Oakville.
Nerantzis, I. 2001. *Η Χώρα των Αιτωλών (Συμβολή στη Γεωπολιτική της Οργάνωση)*. Rethimno.
Novaro, D. 1999. I modellini fittili della tomba di Kamilari: Il problema cronologico, in La Rosa, V., Palermo, D. and Vagnetti, L. (eds) *Επί πόντον πλαζόμενοι, Simposio Italiano di Studi Egei dedicato a Luigi Bernabo Brea e Giovanni Pugliese Carratelli, Roma 18-20, Febbraio 1998*: 151-161. Roma.
Onasoglou, A. 1995. *Η οικία του τάφου των τριπόδων στις Μυκήνες* (Βιβλιοθήκη της εν Αθήναις Αρχαιολογικής Εταιρείας, n.147). Athens.

Palaima, G.Th. 2004. Sacrificial Feasting in the Linear B Documents. *Hesperia* 73: 133-178.
Papadopoulou Zapheiropoulou, F. 1965. Αρχαιότητες και μνημεία Κυκλάδων. Νάξος, ΑΔ 20: 515-522.
Papalexandrou, N. 2008. Boiotian Tripods. The tenacity of a Panhellenic Symbol in A Regial Context. *Hesperia* 77: 251-282.
Papapostolou, A.I. 2009. *Θέρμος: Το μέγαρο Β και το πρώιμο ιερό. Η ανασκαφή 1992-2003* (Βιβλιοθήκη της εν Αθήναις Αρχαιολογικής Εταιρείας). Αθήνα.
Pappi, E. 2014. Ταφικές πρακτικές της Γεωμετρικής Εποχής στο Άργος. Unpublished PhD dissertation. University of Athens, available from: http://thesis.ekt.gr/thesisBookReader/id/40375#page/1/mode/2up
Parker Pearson, M. 1993. The Powerful dead. Archaeological Relationships between the Living and the Dead. *Cambridge Archaeological Journal* 3, Issue 2 October 1993: 203-229, published online: 22 December 2008, available from: http://users.clas.ufl.edu/davidson/arch%20of%20death/Week%2015/Parker%20Pearson%201993.pdf
Popham, R.M., Sackett, H.L. and Themelis, G.P. (eds) 1979. *Lefkandi I, The Iron Age Settlement, (Plates) The Cemeteries*. Oxford.
Popham, R.M., Sackett, H.L. and Themelis, G.P. (eds) 1980. *Lefkandi I, The Iron Age Settlement, (Text) The Cemeteries*. Oxford.
Popham, R.M. and Lemos, S.I. 1996. *Lefkandi III: The Toumba Cenmetery. The excavations of 1981, 1984, 1986 and 1992-1994: Plates*. Oxford.
Rethemiotakis, G. and Egglezou, M. 2010. *Το Γεωμετρικό Νεκροταφείο της Έλτυνας* (Αρχαιολογικό Ινστιτούτο Κρητολογικών Σπουδών 4). Iraklio.
Sánchez Romero, M., Aranda Jiménez, G. and Alarcón García, E. 2007. Gender and age identities in rituals of comensality. The argaric societies, in Interpreting household practices Barcelona, 21-24 November 2007 Treballs d'Arqueologia 13:69-89, available from: https://www.webgea.es/doc/Pub_Treballs13.pdf
Ruiz-Gálvez, M. & Galán, E. 2012. A meal fit for a hero. On the origins of roasted meat, spits and the male ideal, in Aubet, M.E. and Sureda, P. (coordinatores) *Interaccion social y comercio en la antesala del colonialismo, Actes del seminario internacional celebrado en la Universidad Pompeu Fabra el 28 y 29 de Marzo de 2012:* 43-69, available from: https://www.academia.edu/7787964/A_meal_fit_for_a_hero._On_the_origins_of_roasted_meat_spits_and_the_male_ideal._Ruiz-G%C3%A1lvez_and_Gal%C3%A1n
Sherratt, S. 2004. Feasting in Homeric Epic. *Hesperia* 73: 301-337, available from: https://www.academia.edu/2163669/Feasting_in_Homeric_epic
Stavropoulou-Gatsi, M., Jung, R. and Mehofer, M. 2012. Τάφος 'Μυκηναίου' Πολεμιστή στον Κουβαρά Αιτωλοακαρνανίας, in *ATHANASIA, The Earthly, The Celestial and the Underworld in the Mediterranean from the Late Bronze and the Early Iron Age, International Archaeological Conference, Rhodes 28-31 May 2009*: 247-264. Irakleio.
Steel, L. 2004. A Goodly Feast... A Cup of Mellow Wine: Feasting in Bronze Age Cyprus, in *Hesperia* 73:281-300.
Stockhammer, P.W. 2008. Kontinuität und Wandel – DieKeramik der Nachpalastzeit aus der Unterstadt von Tiryns. PhD Dissertation. Heidelberg

University, available at: https://www.researchgate.net/profile/Philipp_Stockhammer/publication/33429206_Kontinuitat_und_Wandel_-_Die_Keramik_der_Nachpalastzeit_aus_der_Unterstadt_von_Tiryns/links/55e8182f08ae65b638996d9a/Kontinuitaet-und-Wandel-Die-Keramik-der-Nachpalastzeit-aus-der-Unterstadt-von-Tiryns.pdf

Stockhammer, P. 2009. The Change of Pottery's Social Meaning at the End of the Bronze Age: New Evidence from Tiryns, in Bachhuber, C. and Roberts, G.R. (eds) *Forces of Transformation: The End of the Bronze Age in the Mediterranean* (Themes from the Ancient Near East BANEA Publication Series 1): 164–169. Oxford.

Węcowski, M. 2009. Greece in the making and the Polis, review of Robin Osborne, Greece in the Making, 1200–479 B.C. (second edition). *Palamedes* 4: 167–176. London – New York, available from: https://www.academia.edu/741257/Review_GREECE_IN_THE_MAKING_AND_THE_POLIS

Węcowski, M. 2011. Symposion, or drinking together. The Rise of the Greek aristocratic banquet (9th to 7th century B.C.) Sub Lupa Press, Warszawa 2011, in Polish (2nd ed). Warszawa. (english summary available from: https://www.academia.edu/780796/Symposion_or_drinking_together._The_rise_of_the_Greek_aristocratic_banquet_9th_to_7th_century_B.C._

Węcowski, M. 2012. When did the SYMPOSION rise? Some archaeological considerations regarding the emergence of the Greek aristocratic banquet. Αρχαιογνωσία 16 (2010-2012):19-48. Athens.

Węcowski, M. 2014. *The Rise of the Greek Aristocratic Banquet*. Oxford University Press. Oxford.

Whitley, J. 1991. Social Diversity in Dark Age Greece. *The Annual of the British School at Athens* 86: 341-365.

Whitley, J. 1991b. *Style and society in Dark Age Greece: The changing face of a pre-literate society 1100-700 BC*. Cambridge.

Whitley, J. 2002. Objects with Attitude: Biographical Facts and Fallacies in the Study of Late Bronze Age and Early Iron Age Warrior Graves. *Cambridge Archaeological Journal* 12:218-232.

Wiessner, P. 1983. Style and Social Information in Kalahari San Projectile Points, in Amerant 48:253-276.

Wright, J.C. 1994. The Spatial Configuration of Belief: The Archaeology of Mycenaean Religion, in Alcock, E.S. and Osborne, R. (eds) *Placing the Gods. Sanctuaries and Sacred Space in Ancient Greece*: 37–78. Oxford.

Wright, J.C. 1995. Empty Cups and Empty Jugs: The Social Role of Wine in Minoan and Mycenaean Societies, in McGovern, E.P., Fleming, J.S. and Katz, H.S. (eds) *The Origins and Ancient History of Wine* (Food and Nutrition in History and Anthropology 11): 287-309. Philadelphia.

Wright, J.C. 1995. From Chief to King in Mycenaean Greece, in Rehak, P. (ed) The Role of the Ruler in the Prehistoric Aegean. Proceedings of a Panel Discussion

Presented at the Annual Meeting of the Archaeological Institute of America, New Orleans Louisiana, 28 December 1992:63-80. With additions. (AEGAEUM 11). Austin, TX: Université de Liège, Histoire de 'art et archéologie de la Grèce antique & University of Texas at Austin, Program in Aegean Scripts and Prehistory. Liege.

Wright, J.C. 2004. A survey of evidence for feasting in Mycenaean society, in *Hesperia* 73:133-178, available from: https://repository.brynmawr.edu/cgi/viewcontent.cgi?referer=&httpsredir=1&article=1005&context=arch_pubs